# COSMOLOGIES
# OF
# CONSCIOUSNESS

# COSMOLOGIES OF CONSCIOUSNESS

Science and Literary Myth
in an Exploration
of the Beginnings
and Development of Mind

**E. C. Barksdale**

SCHENKMAN PUBLISHING CO. INC.
Cambridge, Massachusetts

Copyright© 1980
Schenkman Publishing Company, Inc.
3 Mount Auburn Place
Cambridge, Massachusetts 02138

**Library of Congress Cataloging in Publication Data**

Barksdale, Ethelbert Courtland, 1944-
     Cosmologies of consciousness.

     Bibliography: p.
     Includes index.
     1. Consciousness. 2. Genetic psychology.
3. Mythology. I. Title.
BF311.B286              153              79-23268
ISBN 0-87073-969-7

Printed in the United States of America.

# CONTENTS

v

# PREFACE

Consciousness, a portmanteau term for self-awareness and for those higher brain functions of perception, cognition, logic, memory and imagination, has always been an illusive concept. Although every normal human from early childhood is conscious, psychologists, philosophers, biologists, and theologians have difficulty in defining this universal phenomenon and in dealing with it.

This book takes a relatively new approach to the study of consciousness, beginning with a definition of consciousness based roughly on the movement in philosophy called critical realism and on studies in the school of humanities known as structuralism.

In Part I consciousness is considered as biological fact. Its origins and growth on the planet earth are traced. In Part II some major myths about human consciousness offer insights. The final chapter is concerned with an overview and with implications drawn from this study.

My view of consciousness owes much to conversations with two friends, Dr. Daniel Popp in Scandinavian Studies at The University of Florida, and Mr. David Paul Pace, at that time a student at the University. During our talks Pace argued for the ontological validity of human consciousness, brought to my attention the Tolkien material, and contributed to the development of the fourth stage of the model of the imagination with its immediate, subjective, hypothetical and self-perceiving levels. Professor Popp offered suggestions concerning the application of these concepts to literature. In addition, I am grateful for the continuing support of my colleagues in German and Slavic at the University.

E.C. Barksdale
Spring, 1979

I feel that a man may be happy in this world, and I know that this world is a world of imagination and vision. I see everything I paint in this world, but everybody does not see alike. To the eyes of a miser a guinea is more beautiful than the sun, and the bag worn by the use of money has more beautiful proportions than a vine filled with grapes. The tree which moves some to tears of joy is in the eyes of others only a green thing which stands in the way. Some see Nature all ridicule and deformity, and by these I shall not regulate my proportions: and some scarce see Nature at all. But to the eyes of the man of imagination, Nature is Imagination itself. As a man is, so he sees. As the eye is formed, such are its powers. You certainly mistake when you say that the visions of fancy are not to be found in this world. To me this world is all one continued vision or fancy or imagination. . . .

William Blake

Letter to
Rev. Dr. John Trusler
August 23, 1799[1]

[1]*The Letters of William Blake Together With A Life by Frederick Tatham,* ed. Archibald G. B. Russell (New York: Scribner's, 1906), p. 62.

# PART ONE

## THE SCIENTIFIC ACCOUNT
## OF CONSCIOUSNESS

# CHAPTER I

## CONSCIOUSNESS: A RETROSPECTIVE VIEW

A sunny day on earth many million years in the past was not much different from one in the twentieth century. Ocean waves broke against a rocky coast. On the desert a dust storm was stirring. A meandering stream followed a path outlined by a riverbed, and an animal quenched his thirst there. In the savannahs and in the jungles of the South curious primates were tentatively beginning to explore the world. Toward the North the nights were already cool.

But there was a difference. No conscious mind compared that day with the one before, or made plans for tomorrow, or thought of himself, or of nature, or of any final cause. The drama had no audience.

A day on our planet dawning billions of years ago was warm, too. The earth was host to primitive tropical seas. Clouds drifted across the sky and stars were out at night. Nature had provided a stage where living things would play a brief role and would disappear, but as yet no life had emerged, only a restless stirring, a waiting for the affirmation of being, a pre-science foreshadowing change.

If the scenario were moved back incalculable eons there would be no day, no earth, no sun, only black emptiness, the infinite void. Some twenty-one billion years before this writing, the vast reaches of our universe did not exist. At a time somewhere between fifteen and twenty billion years in the past, all the matter now in the universe was compressed into pinpoint size, or, some think, into nothing at all, and in an infinitesimal second exploded. From the results of that explosion eventually came time and space, the sun, the earth, life, and consciousness.

This study examines the beginnings of the universe and the rise of *Homo sapiens* who has found his place among other forms of matter, inanimate and animate, through the power of his conscious mind. Scientific studies of the development of human consciousness as a physical system are synthesized with literary myths dealing with aspects of consciousness not encompassed by science — the non-cognitive channels of the emotions.

Man possesses multi-layered consciousness. He knows that he exists and that he is different from the world surrounding him. He displays the higher thought processes — perception, cognition, logic, reason, volition, memory, and imagination, that element of mind which has enabled him to become a creative being. As the human developed, he acquired ability to summon up a private, subjective world, to create fantasy, and to project a hypothetical future which may or may not happen. He today is able to experience consciousness on many levels simultaneously, to entertain a concept of himself, and to detach himself from that concept so that he can objectively view himself both as subject and as object. Furthermore, he can project thoughts as independent entities apart from his awareness of self. The center of this study is an examination of the history and development of human consciousness.

A history of human consciousness which bases the development of life and awareness of self on biological facts alone would be incomplete. A series of evaluative statements on that most subjective and personal possession of every human being — his consciousness — without reference to facts would be inadequate. This chronicle must therefore unfold in two different registers: biological and anthropological data of consciousness, the continuum of facts: and emotional assessments concerning the nature of being through which humans have fleshed out the contributions of science in the field of consciousness. The second part of the story is concerned with myth in which the logic of the emotions and of subjectivity interprets and makes more understandable the scientific account. In the last chapter an attempt is made to synthesize the scientific and mythic accounts of consciousness.

# CHAPTER II

## APPROACHES TO CONSCIOUSNESS

A consideration of the relationship between mind and matter reveals many differences separating the physical and mental phenomena of the universe. The human thinks. Apparently the physical world does not. The human exhibits self-awareness. The physical world does not. The human mind is spaceless. Physical objects the size of molecules and larger have spatial locations. Mind can deal with abstractions, such as liberty, hate, and love. The physical world does not entertain conceptions. Since ancient times philosophers in the West have pondered the paradox that the human being has a physical body and hence belongs to the material universe. The mind with its sphere of operations in the human nervous system, especially in the brain, is material. Yet the mind is immaterial in its a-spatial abilities. Philosophers have debated this question through the years under the heading "The Mind/Body Problem."[1]

Idealists believe that mind is transcendent over matter, which, they say, is a passive container or trap for the mind. The eighteenth century Irish idealist George Berkeley held that the physical world is merely a projection of the mind. Materialists consider mind as only another member of the physical world. Epiphenomenalists of the nineteenth century argued that mind is a by-product of molecular action in the brain. A twentieth century correlation variation of the identity hypothesis posits that mind is a correlate of brain states. The theory does not claim that brain states always cause mind states, for at times consciousness controls the brain.

[1] For a survey of the mind/body problem see Jerome Shaffer, *Philosophy of Mind* (Englewood Cliffs, N.J.: Prentice-Hall, 1968).

Alternate solutions to the mind/body problem have been offered. Proponents of naturalism see mind and body as mutually interacting entities. Advocates of a dual-aspect theory believe that mind and matter are two parts of the same system. Neutral monists maintain that both mind and body compose a third concept, experience or sensation. Occasionalists view mind and body as discrete entities which God in his grace links temporarily any time any human being has any thought, profound or trivial.

No solution of the mind/body problem has gained universal acceptance. Idealists can insist that the brain is a receptacle for mind. Materialists can hold that brain is a lump of matter which thinks. No one can prove conclusively that either position is correct. For the mind/body problem to be solved, more must be known about what goes on in the brain when humans have the experience called thinking. A step toward an eventual solution may lie in an understanding of human consciousness. Recent advances in the physical and life sciences, in paleopsychology, and in the study of mythology have contributed a body of data concerning the origin, growth and development of those structures which have undergirded the evolution of the conscious mind and have guided its course through the long ages during which life acquired consciousness.

In the absence of a complete explanation of the mind/body problem, no certain criterion has been formulated to distinguish at what point matter becomes mind. A convenient approach to the question is to accept, for the sake of argument, the proposal of the French anthropologist and philosopher Claude Lévi-Strauss that both the mental and the physical in the universe have an underlying logic, a matrix of organization which can be studied in terms of changes in the patterns which underlie them. Lévi-Strauss writes:

> Beyond the rational there exists a more important and valid category — that of the meaningful, which is the highest mode of being of the rational. . . . I came to the conclusion that beings and things could retain their separate values without losing the clarity of outline which defines them in relationship to each other and gives an intelligible structure to each. Knowledge is based neither on renunciation nor on barter: it consists rather

in selecting *true* aspects, that is, those coinciding with the properties of my thought. Not, as the neo-Kantians claimed, because my thought exercises an inevitable influence over things, but because it is itself an object. Being "of this world," it partakes of the same nature as the world.[2]

If thought can be studied as dispassionately as can any other object, the process by which matter becomes mind can be seen as a structural interchange which began eons ago and which continues today in a reciprocal ecosystem, earth and plants providing oxygen as fuel used by humans who eat plants and herbivorous animals in order to convert food into energy. Thus plants directly or indirectly provide the material food stuffs out of which consciousness is built. Carl Sagan writes:

> Eating is so common that we forget what an extraordinary process it is. We eat corn flakes, and yet, we do not *become* corn flakes. The corn flakes are changed into *us*. In [the California Institute of Technology physicist Richard L.] Feynman's splendid phrase, "Today's brains are yesterday's mashed potatoes."[3]

One of the principal puzzles in tracing life from its unconscious beginnings to higher forms of percipience is the complexity of the intermediate stages between the inanimate and the animate species (for example, viruses) and between minimally conscious organisms and those exhibiting higher forms of life. Clearer boundaries can be drawn, says the Austro-English philosopher of science Sir Karl Popper, if one considers how the universe goes about doing its business. In Popper's view, life itself effects changes in the inertia of the inanimate universe, but conscious life solves problems and knows that they are being solved. Popper categorizes the results of these activities under three headings: the subjective, which is not physical and which makes up the private, inner, a-spatial world of each human: the physical, which consists of public objects extended in space: and the cultural area, which

[2]*Tristes tropiques* (Paris: Plon, 1955), trans. John Weightman and Doreen Weightman (New York: Athenium, 1974: paperback ed. rpt. New York: Pocket Books, 1977), pp. 47-48.

[3]Original comment of Carl Sagan in I. S. Shklovskii, *Vselennaya, zhizn, razium* (1962), trans. Paula Fern and rev. Carl Sagan as *Intelligent Life in the Universe* (San Francisco: Holden-Day, 1966), p. 185.

includes not only "problems and theories and critical arguments," but also "mistakes, myths, stories, witticisms, tools, and works of art."[4] These texts, as Lévi-Strauss would call them, are both mental, in the sense that they were first entertained privately and subjectively by a single human being, and physical, in that they become public and objective in the physical world and are stored in forms such as, for example, books, implements, scores of music, films, statues, computer programs, phonograph records, and intricately designed buildings. These works of ingenuity and of art are seen as the objective results of subjective processes. The universe, not as it potentially might have been, but as it actually *is*, has produced objective consciousness on this planet.

Contrary to the arguments of certain pre-twentieth century vitalists, the appearance of consciousness may be explained without access to extra ingredients existing in life but not in inanimate objects. Popper writes:

> I conjecture that there is no biological process which cannot be regarded as correlated in detail with a physical process or cannot be progressively analyzed in physiochemical terms. But no physiochemical theory can explain the emergence of a new problem, and no physiochemical process can as such solve a problem. . . . *The problems of organisms . . . are specific biological realities; they are "real" in the sense that their existence may be the cause of biological effects.* . . . Life, as we know it, consists of physical "bodies" (more precisely, structures) which are problem solving.
>
> Thus men like Butler and Bergson, though I suppose utterly wrong in their theories, were right in their intuition. Vital force does, of course, exist — but it is in its turn a product of life, *of selection*, rather than anything like the "essence" of life. It is indeed the preferences *which lead the way*. . . . We need not assume that these preferences are conscious. But they may become conscious: . . .
>
> My approach, therefore, leads almost necessarily to a research programme that asks for an explanation, in objective biological terms, of the emergence of states of consciousness.[5]

[4]"Autobiography," in Karl Popper et al. *The Philosophy of Karl Popper*, ed. Paul Arthur Schilpp (La Salle, Ill.: Open Book Publishing Company, 1974), I, 148, 151.

[5]Ibid., pp. 142-43.

In the chapters which follow, the beginnings of Popper's requested objective history of consciousness will be supplied, but it will be objective biological history only insofar as a scientific account can, given the present state of knowledge, be achieved. Many reductionist materialists maintain that science will some day completely account for consciousness with its volition, conceptualization, and imagination, by reference to brain processes alone. Such a one-to-one, conscious-state-to-brain-state explanation is not possible now — if it ever will be.

While science deals only with natural phenomena, mythology includes supernatural as well as natural planes of existence. Science seeks to account for actual or potential events and relationships. Mythology deals with unproved assumptions. It has been argued that every science contains mythic elements in that every new scientific hypothesis is a conjecture which has not yet been squared with the facts. Every scientist yearns to prove his latest hypothesis as quickly as possible by demonstrating that his theory is congruent with the reality of fact.

Not so the mythmaker. The assumptions of the myth may be substantiated by facts, but far more often myth comes from another source, from metaphysics, religion, or folk beliefs. Ultimately, the verity of a myth is a revealed truth. It is contained in the myth itself which is, in turn, a part of a belief system, complete, or assumed to be complete, in order for the myth to be effective. Most scientific treatises are concerned with postulated objective data. Scientists, when new and contradictory information appears, change a belief system in order to align the new certainty more closely with proved research. In mythmaking, facts are conceptualized or bent so that they will conform more closely with the belief system.

In literate cultures myths have come to be incorporated in works of literature. Not all scientific and not all myth-influenced literary texts deal with consciousness, but some mythmakers and some scientists are centrally concerned with it. After a consideration of the findings in science in this area, several outstanding mytho-literary texts are examined to provide further insight into the origin and the development of consciousness.

# CHAPTER III

## THE PRELUDE TO LIFE

Given present knowledge, the question of the origin of the universe is still a metaphysical one. Philosophers postulate that the universe had no beginning. Most astronomers today assume that the *physical* universe, *as we know it*, originated in a split second between fifteen and twenty billion years ago when all the matter in the universe was compressed into an area about the size of the head of a pin, or, in some physicists' theories, to a point in space.[1] Where the matter was before that minute occurred, scientists cannot say. The material of the huge shrinkage and compression to miniscule size may have been the remains of a universe which had existed at some time earlier. But at a point fifteen to twenty billion years ago, all of the universe was contracted into a tiny space, creating a tremendous amount of potential energy. Suddenly a cosmos-shaking explosion, rather ineloquently called by astronomers the *big bang*, happened. The ultimate fate of that matter is not known. One theory which is gaining converts among astronomers is that the matter in the universe was so pushed by the immensity of the explosion that it will go on expanding toward infinity forever and will never contract.[2]

Startling proof of the validity of the big bang theory of the origin of the present universe came in the 1960's in the discovery of the record of sound left by the cosmic explosion. This

---

[1]See P. C. W. Davies, *Space and Time in the Modern Universe* (Cambridge: Cambridge Univ. Press, 1977), pp. 159-60.

[2]The theory is described by the Harvard University astronomer Owen Gingrich, "Will the Universe End with a Bang or a Whimper?" *Harvard Magazine*, 79, No. 2 (July-Aug., 1977), 10.

phenomenon may be compared to known data, the movement of light. When a human views a star, he is seeing only the past record of that body. So vast is the universe that the light which left the star has taken years, for quite distant stars billions of years, to reach the human eye. The image on the retina tells the observer how the planet appeared when the light first began its journey. Just as light finally reaches the eye, the sound of the big bang has travelled billions of years so that the astronomer listening now is actually hearing the birth of the universe.

In the early 1960's Robert H. Dicke of Princeton University had predicted that some form of radiation caused by the original big bang might be found. In 1965 two communication engineers at the Bell Telephone laboratories, A. A. Penzias and R. W. Wilson, were at first annoyed by background static which kept interfering with their attempts to signal communication satellites. They pointed a horn-reflector antenna at all points in the sky and found the noise everywhere. If Dicke's theory is correct, the sound is an omnipresent echo of the big bang.[3]

A few seconds after the explosion, plan was evident in the universe. A *plan* is an unconscious pattern which guides activities. Plan differs from a *goal* in that the latter is the result of *conscious* plan. Many activities of the universe appear to be very loosely planned. They seem almost completely random. Some scientists and philosophers believe that, following the laws of thermodynamics, the universe will some day become totally random in its workings.

Scientists and philosophers who argue for plan in the universe often base their case on the fact that life has developed. The phenomenon of life is proof that the universe manifests a capacity for organization higher than would be possible if the actions of the universe were governed only by chance. If, however, one accepts the thesis that the universe may be infinite, possibility exists that chance alone could produce life. Some scientists, although they are now in a minority, contend that the development of life itself shows no evidence of plan.

---

[3]For a discussion of Dicke's theory and the work of Wilson and Penzias, see William J. Kaufmann, III, *Relativity and Cosmology* (New York: Harper & Row, 1973), pp. 116-17.

Jacques Monod believes that life is the result of random combination of invariant molecules.[4] Many scientists today agree with the position presented here that evolution in life is governed by variations, the occurrence of which are occasioned by probabilities greater than blind chance. The type of plan proposed here is a highly plastic one in which chance has an enormous play. In a universe completely governed by chance, it is extremely unlikely that life and consciousness would exist. The presence of life and consciousness constitutes a counter-argument to the thesis that the universe is totally random.

Two illustrations indicate the difference between a world governed by chance and one in which plan operates. An inebriated person proceeding around a jogging course is not governed by plan. He will move this way and that way. He may turn around and change directions. He may leave the course and run in the grass adjacent to the track. His motions are what statisticians call random. No probabilities can be offered as to what his next move will be.

A log floating down a river provides an example of plan. The log has no conscious goal but the chances are, unless, for example, the log is stuck on a mud bar, that it will continue to move in the direction in which it is presently floating. The movement of the log is not absolutely certain, but it is highly probable. Its motion is governed not by goal but by plan.

At the moment of the big bang, plan was functioning in the universe in a significant way. The British radio-astronomer Sir Bernard Lovell writes:

> It is a remarkable fact that the existence even of stars and galaxies depends in a delicate manner on the force of attraction between two protons [sub-atomic particles]. In the earliest moments of the expansion of the universe, a millionth of a second after the beginning, calculations indicate that the temperature was of the order ten million million degrees and the fundamental particles of nature—protons, neutrons, electrons and hyperons — existed with radiation as the controlling force. One second after the beginning, when the temperature had fallen to a few thousand million degrees, there was a critical period when the natural constants determined the ultimate abundance of

[1]See Jacques Monod, *Le Hassard et la nécessité* (Paris: Éditions du Seuil, 1970).

helium to hydrogen in the universe. The existence of hydrogen is vital to the evolution of stars and galaxies — the sun and the stars generate their energy by the thermonuclear transformation of hydrogen to helium. It is an astonishing reflection that at this critical early moment in the history of the universe, all of the hydrogen would have turned into helium if the force of attraction between protons — that is, the nuclei of hydrogen atoms — had been only a few per cent stronger. In the earliest stages of the expansion of the universe, the primeval condensate would have turned into helium. No galaxies, no stars, no life would have emerged. It would have been a universe forever unknowable by living creatures. A remarkable and intimate relationship **between man, the fundamental constants of nature, and the** initial moments of space and time seems to be an inescapable condition of our existence.[5]

No physicist has offered reasons for the existence of plan although theists do not hesitate to enter where physicists have yet to tread. In the 1970's the Cambridge University astronomer Fred Hoyle revived the ideas of the nineteenth century physicist Ernst Mach who said that the inertial properties of each particle of matter are determined by the properties in all other matter. In Mach's scheme the incredibly small subatomic particle, the proton, gains its mass from the distribution of the rest of the matter in the universe. Hoyle asks:

> How then are we to understand everyday experience? By recognizing that our everyday world is not truly local. We are not in fact separated from the universe in the large. Causality arises not locally but from an interaction with the whole universe. Indeed it is the universe in the large that impresses causality on our everyday world.[6]

Regardless of what reasons for causality may eventually be discovered, plan existed from the first second of the history of the universe. But it was plastic and capable of changing as conditions changed.

---

[5]"Whence?" *The New York Times Magazine* (16 Nov., 1975), p. 88. Not all astronomers agree that there is such a strong dependence between life and the first moments of the universe. See Davies, *Space and Time in the Modern Universe*, pp. 211-212.

[6]"The Crisis in Astronomy," *Physics 50 Years Later*, ed. Sanborn C. Brown (Washington, D.C.: National Academy of Sciences, 1973), p. 77.

Immediately after the big bang, enough cooling took place to allow the presence of stable helium and hydrogen, but most of the cosmos was still in the form of radiation energy.[7] Seven hundred thousand years after its inexplicable beginning, the universe reached a critical point. It was large enough that the effects of the big bang had begun slowly to diminish. Tiny particles of dust, products of hydrogen and helium, filled the universe. The gaseous material was at first distributed evenly, but each modicum of dust was attracted to every other one by gravity. With the cooling of the universe, this action slowed. Eventually, as determined by statistical probability, currents of fluctuating matter coagulated. The huge eddies which appeared a few billions years after the big bang are called galaxies. Today galaxies are still in the making as stars continue to form.[8]

Stars are made when a critical level for initiating fusion is reached. It takes approximately a billion trillion trillion atoms to constitute a galaxy. These condensations of matter cause atoms to coalesce and produce tremendous amounts of friction in the form of heat. The protons — hydrogen nuclei — become so hot that they smash together, fusing into the double proton nuclei of helium atoms. The stars are giant furnaces with hydrogen as fuel and helium as ash.[9] As hydrogen turns into helium, and ever greater amounts of heat and light are released, a star is born. For billions of years, while it has fuel, the star sends out enormous amounts of heat and light over millions of miles. On earth such heat and light, now at "tolerable" levels, constitute sunshine.

Some five billion years ago, an ordinary star in our galaxy (which is called the Milky Way) was forming. That star is our sun. As it spewed out matter, heat and light, it also became a powerful center of gravitation, pulling space dust toward it.

---

[7]For a brief discussion of cosmology see Eric J. Chaisson, "The Scenario of Cosmic Evolution," *Harvard Magazine*, 80, No. 2 (Nov.-Dec., 1977), 21-33. A fuller treatment is D. W. Sciama, *Modern Cosmology* (Cambridge: Cambridge Univ. Press, 1971).

[8]Chaisson, "The Scenario of Cosmic Evolution," p. 23.

[9]For a popular account of the origin of the stars, see Isaac Asimov, *The Universe: From Flat Earth to Quasar* (New York: Walker, 1966: paperback ed. New York: Avon Books, 1966), pp. 149-50.

Many heavier chemicals — oxygen, magnesium, iron, silicon, and sulphur, which had been synthesized in stars far more massive than the sun — were contained in the space dust. Even heavier bits of metal, such as nickel, tin, bismuth, gold and uranium, which had been formed in the destruction of a type of star called a supernovas, were in the dust.[10]

With the eviction of gas, heat, and light, the sun was also pushing out large eddies of flat disks of interstellar gases and dust which contained bits of all the elements which were soon to make up our earth.[11] As these disks coalesced into great rounded lumps called planets, plan continued to be present. Too small to escape the sun's gravity and float away, and too large to be pulled back into the sun, the disks moved around the sun. By approximately four and six-tenths billion years ago, a planet called earth was in orbit around the sun.

Initially, because the surface of the earth had been so hot that most material boiled away and escaped as gas, no atmosphere could form. When the surface of the earth had cooled so that it could tolerate a primitive atmosphere, heavy rainstorms occurred which eventually formed great, warm, tropical oceans. This was the scene of the first life on our planet.

---

[10]Chaisson, "The Scenario of Cosmic Evolution," p. 27.
[11]Ibid., p. 28.

# CHAPTER IV

## THE PROGRAM OF LIFE

In the mid-nineteenth century, Louis Pasteur, in a series of experiments with sterile nutrient broth, proved that no organism can be formed out of inanimate matter on earth *as the earth now exists.*[1] But on the earth three billion years ago, conditions were different. Most scientists now believe that around that time living forms appeared out of inanimate matter. The theory of the conversion of inanimate to animate matter was first proposed in the 1920's by the Soviet biologist A. I. Oparin and was given wide hearing in the 1930's after the publication of Oparin's book *The Origin of Life on Earth.*[2] In 1953, Stanley L. Miller, then a student of Harold C. Urey at the University of Chicago, re-created in the laboratory a small-scale version of primitive conditions on earth. Organic compounds, essential ingredients for life, were formed in a bell jar. The result of these experiments offered dramatic proof that Oparin's thesis was correct.

Scientists do not know precisely when life began or the exact stages between the origin of organic compounds and the appearance of life. A key to the problem may come when it is known how DNA (DNA is short for *d*ioxyribo*n*ucleic *a*cid) was first formed. Before the appearance of DNA, compounds called amino acids had been produced by a system operating

---

[1] For an account of Pasteur's work see William T. Keeton, *Biological Science*, 2nd ed. (1967: New York: Norton, 1972), p.46.

[2] Oparin's thesis was first stated in Aleksandr I. Oparin, *Proizkhozhdenie zhizni* [*The Origin of Life*] (Moscow: Izd. Moskovsky rabochy. 1924). It was made prominent by a second book, Aleksandr I. Oparin, *Vozniknovenie zhizni na zemle* (1936; 3rd ed. 1956), trans. Ann Synge as *The Origin of Life on Earth* (New York: Academic Press, 1957).

with probabilities significantly higher than chance. Plan was therefore present, but the first forms of life possessed more than plan. They had a *program*, a special kind of plan. They had no goals because they did not exhibit consciousness. Living things, according to S. I. Luria, are the only entities now known in the universe which have a program.[3] When the DNA molecule first took over cell maintenance and the reproduction of organisms, a program was established.

The program which governs life insures that life will be expressed over and over again in countless individual organisms. Though the individuals die, the program is passed on. It provides a second guarantee — that no single organism will be exactly like any other organism.Differences are sometimes marginal, but every individual is in some ways unique.

Organic compounds on the primitive earth were succeeded by unicellular organisms during a period from over three billion to two and a half billion years ago. Multicellular organisms evolved a billion years ago. Between the establishment of inanimate matter and the first living substances, protein-like substances which ate, ejected wastes, grew, reproduced, and died were found, but they as yet had no DNA, the master programing material which all modern forms of life possess.[4]

The question of how DNA was formed can best be approached by considering the role of DNA in organisms today. A model for DNA was first proposed in the 1950's by John D. Watson and Francis Crick, both then working at Cambridge. DNA, a complex organic molecule, is present in every cell of every living organism on earth. As factors in the cell deteriorate, the cell replaces worn-out parts, particularly proteins, by taking in food and fuel. The cell is thus a chemical factory which builds specific proteins. The cell burns food which it changes to more simple components in order to keep alive.

DNA, the master molecule which structures life, interacts with another chemical RNA *(ribonucleic acid)*. RNA lines up certain chemicals — the twenty amino acids which make up proteins in foods — in order to form materials needed to build

[3] S. I. Luria, *Life: The Unfinished Experiment* (New York: Scribner's, 1973), pp.5-6.
[4] Chaisson, "The Scenario of Cosmic Evolution," pp.28-29.

new cells. Each of the bases in RNA is arranged by DNA. The amino acids are in turn arranged by RNA. If each of the amino acids is considered a letter in the alphabet, DNA may be called the code book of life because DNA lines up the chemicals which form life's blueprint.

When new cells are produced, DNA must be passed on to each of them. DNA splits exactly in half. Each half acts as a template against which a new half is forged. The cell now contains twice as much DNA. Half of that double dose is passed on to a new cell. At the end of the process, two cells have replaced one. Each new cell has an identical amount of DNA.

If all cells contained only the same kind of DNA, life would consist of only one kind of one-celled creatures. For reasons not yet clear, different kinds of cells evolve. Multi-celled entities change into more complex forms of life. In one-celled organisms, reproduction occurs by simple splitting of the cells. In most higher organisms, specialized reproductive cells exist. In these cells the DNA making up the units of heredity called genes is arranged on chromosomes, tiny thread-like substances. Through a complicated series of stages, each parent provides half of the genetic material for the offspring. According to the laws of heredity, in each pair of chromosomes in the offspring, one member of the two predominates and passes on a group of traits. A complete explanation for the diversification is not yet available, but some factors causing changes in organization have been isolated.

Although each member of each species has the same number of chromosomes, no two members are exactly alike. On the contrary, a part of the program of life guarantees that every organism is different. The factor of plasticity occurs in RNA's deliberate "misreading" of the pattern of DNA when RNA lines up the proteins to produce different individuals.

In 1966 Harry Harris of the University of London and Richard Lewontin and John Hubby of the University of Chicago traced the electron activity which takes place in the building of the amino acids. They found that when proteins are being synthesized, misreading the code is quite common. Exceptions occur in unicellular organisms and in multicellular identical twins (which begin to differentiate only after a cell produced by sexual reproduction is already formed, and hence are alike in basic proteins). All other organisms are so different that two humans in the same family (unless they are identical twins) differ to a degree far greater than does the entire human species from chimpanzees.[5] Even identical twins are not alike. The location of certain organs is normal in one twin and is reversed in the other. The direction of coil in spiral organs is reversed. Identical twins are misnamed. They are as unlike as are right and left hands. They are mirror images of each other.[6]

In 1976, Francis Crick, together with Aaron Klug, Sydney Brenner, and George Pieczenik, proposed that when life first appeared on earth, each RNA molecule was linked with five bases rather than with the three bases which is now the case.[7] With five bases, each RNA molecule could control one amino acid directly. RNA was first seen in tiny granules of proteins called ribosomes, but Crick's team has proposed that three and two-tenths billion years ago RNA may have appeared without ribosomes.

If this theory is correct, proteins and RNA must have led the way to the formation of DNA, but once DNA was formed, it became the controlling factor of life. Pieczenik says that it is DNA, not the organism, which counts in the life process, and that evolution in Darwin's sense could not have been initiated until organisms were formed.

Pieczenik's ideas would at first seem to lend credence to a new theory named by Harvard's Edward O. Wilson, *sociobiology*.[8] Sociobologists argue that such traits as aggression

---

[5] For a discussion of Lewontin and Hubby, see Nigel Calder, *The Life Game* (1973: paperback ed. rpt. New York:Dell, 1975), pp.19-21.

[6] On identical twins as mirror images of each other, see Paul A. Weiss, *The Science of Life* (Mount Kisco, N.Y.: Futura Publishing Co., 1973),pp.43-44.

[7] F. H. C. Crick et al. "A Speculation on the Origin of Protein Synthesis," *Origins of Life*, 7 (1976), 389-97.

[8] The original full treatment of sociobiology is Edward O. Wilson, *Sociobiology* (Cambridge: Harvard Univ. Press, 1975). For an opposing view which stresses that human social organizations, unlike organizations of lower animals, are not principally controlled by heredity, see Marshall Sahlins, *The Use and Abuse of Biology* (Ann Arbor: Univ. of Michigan Press, 1976).

and altruism are genetically determined in social animals rang-
ing from insects to human beings. But Pieczenik remarks:
"The DNA sequences don't really care if they have to look like
a lowly assistant professor or a giraffe."[9] The views of
sociobiologists are very controversial, especially when the findings are applied to human beings. Lewontin believes, for instance, that the plastic nervous system possessed by human
beings mitigates against such predeterminism as
sociobiologists would have it. Marvin Harris states that
sociobiologists tend to underestimate drastically the novelty in
evolution which produces human culture; Harris believes that
learning can be passed on to the members of the culture,
thereby overwhelming any genetic contribution to behavior.[10]

The controversy between sociobiologists and their oppo-
nents is in a way but another chapter in the ancient conflict of
nature versus nurture, heredity versus environment. Wilson
himself admits that only ten to fifteen per cent of human
behavior is genetically based, but sociobiologists emphasize
that this is an important ten to fifteen per cent.[11] Most geneti-
cists, biologists, anthropologists, and psychologists today take a
position that falls between the two extremes of those who, like
the sociobiologists, argue that human activities are in major
ways controlled by heredity, and those who, like the
psychologist B. F. Skinner, maintain that human behavior is
almost totally the product of the environment.

John Maynard Smith of Sussex University views evolution as
game theory in which various species adopt strategy based
both on heredity and environment, a combination which will
help to insure the species' chances of survival.[12] C. H. Waddington has shown that the relationship between genes and
environment is a program, a plastic plan in which the activity of
the genes is modified by feedback from the environment.
Genes do not react with the environment according to the

---

[9] Quoted in the Editors of *Time*, "Why You Do What You Do," *Time*, 110, No. 5 (Aug. 1, 1977), 55.

[10] Ibid., p. 58.

[11] Ibid.

[12] For a discussion of John Maynard Smith's theory of species survival, see Calder, *The Life Game*, pp.58-68.

analogy of a random walk. Neither do they behave with complete certainty. Life moves in weighed directions which with each move close off numerous possible streams of development, but, at the same time, open other alternatives.[13]

Many questions remain unanswered concerning both the origin of living species, the nature of their development, and the plan which guides on-going life. Nonetheless, unicells first and then more complex organisms did appear on the earth. They did begin to evolve, and eventually conscious organisms appeared.

---

[13] For a full account of Waddington's thesis, see C.H. Waddington, *The Strategy of the Genes* (New York: Macmillan, 1957). For a brief discussion see C.H. Waddington, "The Theory of Evolution Today," in *Beyond Reductionism*, ed. Arthur Koestler and J.M. Smythes (New York: Macmillan, 1969), pp. 357-99.

# CHAPTER V

## THE COMING OF MAN

The conscious organism displays the higher brain processes and possesses self-awareness. Some lower animals exhibit rudimentary evidence of perception, cognition, and logic integrated into complex, well-organized systems. None possess brains with the character and sophistication human brains have achieved, and none, so far as is known, are creatures who may be called self-aware. None see themselves as individuals or show knowledge of mortality to the degree which men and women do.

Scientists treat the capacities of realization of self and the abilities involved in reasoning about life and death as the result of a new and more intricate information-processing system which the higher organisms, and especially *Homo sapiens,* have evolved. The birth of consciousness occurred when multicellular organisms appeared. Multicellular organisms became fairly abundant after the beginning of the Cambrian period six hundred million years ago, but some simpler specimens are found to have existed and flourished years before. As the centuries passed, the sea and land were populated with animals. Land-dwelling animals appeared about three hundred million years ago. The more complex animals devoted some of their cells to information-processing alone. They had evolved a nervous system.

The first specialization of nerve cells seems primitive when compared to the capacities of the modern brain of *Homo sapiens.* The "proto-brain" of the earthworm — and it has not changed much in the millions of years that the earth has played host to these creatures — is only a small bulb at one end of the nervous system. The bulb, however, serves as a trigger mechanism to command other nerves to fire in order to cause the earthworm to respond to simple stimuli from the outside world. The earthworm's information-processing system is one-channeled.

When evolution produced vertebrates, organisms with spinal cords and backbones, great improvement had been made. The dinosaurs, a superfamily of vertebrates which ruled the earth around a hundred fifty million years ago, once erroneously considered stupid by researchers, are now thought to have been warm-blooded or a transition group between cold-blooded and warm-blooded animals.[1] The brain of the dinosaur was multi-channeled but was lacking in the critical complexity necessary for the higher brain function which would make self-awareness possible.

The mammals, who nursed their young, made their appearance while the dinosaurs were lords of the planet. At first no more than tiny hairy animals, they separated and differentiated, becoming rodent-like animals who possessed neither of the two criteria necessary for consciousness, but who were able to engage in definite multi-channeled information processing. Small in number of species, they spent most of their lives trying to keep from being eaten by dinosaurs. In order to survive, they had to occupy ecological niches where they would be safe from attack. They became night dwellers who woke after most of the diurnal dinosaurs were asleep. Thus they did not have to compete for survival and were free to scavenge without becoming food for their enemies. At first, mammals had weak eyes, but they developed special optic nerve endings called rods which were adapted for seeing especially well at night.

Needing an additional sense to help them search for game and run from predators, they developed a remarkably sensitive hearing apparatus, one that was stereoscopic or in-depth. There are reptiles who have only one ear below the stomach.

---

[1] The argument that dinosaurs were truly warm-blooded is presented by Adrian J. Desmond, *The Hot-Blooded Dinosaurs* (New York: Dial, 1976). Richard Wasserug argues, citing Armand de Ricqlés, that dinosaurs were a transition type between cold-blooded and warm-blooded animals. See Wasserug, rev. of *The Hot-Blooded Dinosaurs* by Adrian Desmond, *Science*, 193 (1976), 44.

Mammals, however, have two ears, one on each side of the head, enabling them to hear aggressors, no matter how distant, from all directions. In order to achieve stereoscopic hearing, their brain had to be able to process two signals simultaneously, though both belonged to only one sense, that of hearing. The brain grew slightly more complex to handle the increased information load.

The dinosaurs some seventy million years ago disappeared in a short period of time; no reason has been found for their catastrophic demise. Once the dinosaurs were gone, the mammals could conquer the earth and occupy every ecological niche from sea creatures (whales and dolphins) through mammals which fly (bats) to those which live on land (from elephants to horses to rats).

With their new ecological position, mammals became day as well as night animals, evolving more complex eyes so that they could see as readily in daylight as at night. Our chief interest in these mammals is confined to a group of tree dwellers who later ranged the land. Anthropocentrically, they are called primates since man belongs to that group.

The simplest primates, such as the lemur, already possessed two characteristics which were later to aid humans to reach consciousness. The first digit of the paw of the primate became the ancestor of man's opposable thumb which allows man to make tools and other artifacts of a material culture. Primates' eyes were set in their faces (as compared with, for example, the eyes of a horse which are found on each side of the head). The position of the primates' eyes allowed them to develop stereoscopic vision. Additionally, they evolved color vision. These faculties, combined with depth hearing, meant that primates were encoding stereoscopically in two major senses. They became very successful and the primate brain shot ahead of the brains of their competitors.

Modern man belongs to the family *Hominidae*.[2] In the nineteenth and early twentieth centuries, anthropologists instigated a search for a "missing link" between ape and man.

---

[2] Grahame Clark, *A World Prehistory*, 2nd ed. (1961: Cambridge: Cambridge Univ. Press, 1969), p. 6.

Today many scientists agree with anthropologists who have changed Nietzsche's view that man is the link between animal and superman to the notion that modern man is the missing link between the animal and the truly human.[3]

Anthropologists in the twentieth century have unearthed finds which indicate that previous candidates for the missing link, such as Peking man and Java man, are part of a continuum of development. A better understanding of the ascent of man has come from the recent work of many anthropologists, especially the Leakeys — Louis and Mary and their son Richard — whose work has been done in Africa.[4] The record of man is still incomplete, but anthropologists are sure that modern man is a mixture of many stocks, some of which have at times lived together on earth, so that it is no longer possible to set up a scheme for evolution which will proceed from ape to quasi-ape to man. Today one must consider, as new evidence mounts, that many related groups of apes and later of proto-men evolved to produce modern man.

The earliest that anthropologists can go back with certainty into man's simian ancestry is to the ape *Dryopithecus* who evolved some twenty million years ago. The line split into three groups: *Gigantopithecus*, huge round apes which became extinct; *Pongidae*, modern gorillas and chimpanzees; and *Ramapithecus*, appearing between ten and fourteen million years ago. From the *Ramapithecus* group came modern man.

*Ramapithecus* was an ape, but his teeth resembled teeth of man-like hominids rather than those of apes. As climatic conditions changed, Africa, which had been tropical, became colder. Some jungles thinned into plain-like savannahs. Members of the *Ramapithecus* group in subsequent millenia ventured into the savannahs and developed new skills. In order to see above the tall grass, they walked upright.

[3] John E. Pfeiffer, *The Emergence of Man* (New York: Harper & Row, 1969), pp. 4-5.

[4] For the work of the Leakeys see Louis S.B. Leakey, *The Progress and Evolution of Man in Africa* (London: Oxford Univ. Press, 1961), Louis S.B. Leakey and Vanne Morris Goodall, *Unveiling Man's Origins* (Cambridge, Mass. :Schenkman, 1969), and Richard E. Leakey and Roger Lewin, *Origins* (New York: Dutton, 1977). For a general survey of the work of many scientists on human evolution, see Glynn Ll. Isaac and Elizabeth R. McCown, ed. *Human Origins* (Menlo Park, Cal.: Benjamin, 1976).

Between eight and five million years in our past, the savannah-dwelling members of *Ramapithecus* showed marked differences from the forest-dwelling group. Two lines, *Australopithecus robustus* and *Australopithecus africanus* developed. Basically, the Australopithecines were upright, walking apes with small teeth and hair over their bodies. Their skulls were more like skulls of apes than those of men. They did, however, use simple tools.[5]

The Australopithecines were largely foragers rather than hunters. They did not have the skills or the fine brains which were to come much later. Some anthropologists believe that man is a descendant of *Australopithecus africanus*. Others hold that the line which produced man evolved from multiple strands of earlier pre-man around eight to five million years ago. In either case, by two million years in our past, the first beings who belonged to the species *Homo* were not only evolving but were in the ascendancy.

In 1972, Richard Leakey unveiled a skull known as Skull No. 1470 which gave evidence that *Homo sapiens* has existed more than two million years.[6] In 1975, Mary Leakey found a humanoid fossil which dates back some three and a half million years. Richard Leakey's find belongs to a group called *Homo habilis* which was not yet *Homo sapiens*. *Homo habilis* had body hairs like hairs of modern man, but his brain was half the size that modern man would subsequently develop. *Homo habilis* was a hunter and made use of pebbled tools. Gradually the Australopithecines disappeared and the branch *Homo* predominated. Approximately a million and a half years ago, the now extinct branches of *Homo erectus* evolved from the *Homo* genus. Its representatives, such as Java and Peking man, were hominids or proto-men who discovered fire, enjoyed the use of a larger brain, and developed tools of stone. They had heavy ape-like brow ridges and flattened foreheads.[7]

Some three hundred fifty thousand years in our past, the species *Homo sapiens* emerged, but he was not yet modern man.

---

[5]Calder, *The Life Game*, p. 161.
[6]Ibid., pp. 161-63.
[7]Clark, *A World Prehistory*, p. 11.

Early representatives of his line included sub-species *Homo sapiens neanderthalis,* or Neanderthal man. Modern man, now sometimes called *Homo sapiens sapiens* (with *sapiens* written twice to distinguish him from such types as *Homo sapiens neanderthalis)*[8] developed around fifty thousand years ago, and in the subsequent millenia, only modern man of all his ancestors was left on earth.[9]

With the appearance of man came the first creature, and perhaps the only one, who possesses the qualities of full consciousness — the higher brain processes, an awareness of self, and the capacity to formulate goals. Although the chimpanzee exhibits rudimentary signs of language, no chimp has ever spontaneously developed language itself. He is a tool user in the sense that he will sometimes pick up a stick to help him get an object, such as a banana, that he wants. Other lower animals also use tools. The California sea otter brings a boulder up from the botton of the sea and cracks mollusks against it.[10] But no one holds that the sea otter is conscious of what he is doing. The act is for him an intrinsic, instinctual process. The chimp uses different sticks at different times to help him gain objects. Hence his behavior is non-instinctual and shows rudimentary insight. But the effect is not sustained. He never uses the same tool twice or teaches his offspring to use it. It is therefore not tool-using or tool-making which defines man's consciousness. It is rather the characteristics of imagination and memory which enable man to use the same tool over again. What is more, it is the understanding of the symbolic concept *tool* which defines the consciousness of man.[11]

Modern man differs from his predecessors, not only in physical characteristics and in brain size, but also in the possession of symbolic culture in which information is integrated at high levels, encoded in complex ways, and taught to his progeny. With these accomplishments, a new level of culture called

---

[8]Ibid., pp. 10-11.

[9]Calder, *The Life Game,* p. 162.

[10]The sea otter is discussed in W. H. Thorpe, *Learning and Instinct in Animals,* 2nd ed. (1956: Cambridge: Harvard Univ. Press, 1963), p. 121.

[11]Clark, *A World Prehistory,* p. 25.

civilization was initiated. The invention of agriculture, the emergence of art, religion, mathematics, and writing, and the appearance of large cities with vastly different and disparate levels of culture were essential results of full consciousness which must, however, depend upon yet another element — articulate speech.[12] It cannot be proved that speech existed until the invention of writing around five thousand years ago but language surely arose much earlier. It made man human.

---

[12]Ibid., p. 34.

# CHAPTER VI

## THE BREAKTHROUGH TO LANGUAGE

Although the origin of language is unknown, the problem of language beginnings has not been neglected. In the 1860's the Linguistic Society of Paris was so swamped with papers claiming to have discovered the secret of the genesis of language that the Society passed a by-law that anyone attempting to read a paper on the origin of language would automatically be declared out of order.[1] A basic reason that the question has not been solved is that man learned to speak before written records were kept. When writing came into use, many records of previous oral cultures were put into written form.

Spoken language must pre-date the written tongue by thousands of years. Yet one does not know how far back to take the record to the day — if there ever were such a day — when humans had no language. Modern-day apes, chimpanzees and gorillas, man's closest relatives, have well-developed communication systems. The repertory includes not only verbal chatter, but facial expressions and gestures. Many lower animals, such as bees, have fixed and stereotyped signaling systems. Among living things the apes have a far more plastic communication system than representatives on the other end of the plasticity scale. Flowers, for example, have certain odors or colors and thereby attract only certain kinds of bees. No one claims that flowers spontaneously communicate. On the other hand, everyone knows that humans practice spontaneous, varied, and plastic systems of speech supplemented by facial expressions and body gestures. Since all of the higher animals

---

[1]Edgar H. Sturtevant, *An Introduction to Linguistic Science* (New Haven: Yale Univ. Press, 1947), p. 40.

evidence varying degrees of skill in conveying information, it is supposed that apes, around the time that man split off from that line in his evolutionary development, also had some kind of communication system. Whether man at first had such a complex model as he now possesses is not known and there is no evidence — and there may never be any evidence in the future — which will prove the degree of sophistication of early communication patterns.

Even if one assumes that the earliest proto-man had a communication system, modern human speech (and hereafter speech and language will be used as synonyms unless otherwise indicated) is far more complex than communication of any other known species. Language is the result of a confluence of various systems — sound, morphology, syntax, and semantics — together with a lexicon of words and rules for language encoding which are stored in the human memory. The result is a mélange of such complexity that the MIT linguist Noam Chomsky has wondered if language may be beyond the explanatory powers of present-day chemistry and physics.

If language cannot be adequately explained, even more remote is the possibility of a detailed chronology of the development of language which would list the stages by which simple early speech developed into its modern forms. It is fashionable to deride such pre-twentieth century notions that spoken language is based on imitations of lower animals (the "bow-bow" type of theory) or that it arose from expletives (the "ouch-ouch" theory).[2] Nonetheless modern theorists cannot do much better. One of the more perceptive contemporary theories of the development of language comes from the Yale linguist Morris Swadesh who proposes that the sounds of man were first imitative and then exclamatory, with the exclamatory system splitting into two paradigms, the expressive and the demonstrative. At such point, he reasons, man was in the Old Stone Age and could use modified sticks and simple tools.[3]

---

[2] These theories of the origin of language are discussed and ridiculed in John P. Hughes, *The Science of Language* (New York: Random House, 1962), p. 30.

[3] *The Origin and Diversification of Language* (Chicago: Aldine-Atherton, 1971), p. 182.

Swadesh's theory traces the changes in the spoken language from a time when man unthinkingly emitted cries until, as a thinker, he pronounced words. Swadesh does not explain — and no other theorist of the origin of language has been able to do it either — how man achieved what Swadesh calls the "expressive paradigm," the ability to use sounds, not merely as exclamatory grunts or as verbal finger gestures pointing out objects, but also as abstract symbols whereby the world can be modeled. No present-day theory of language tries to explain how language became an indispensable function — and some say the very basis — of human consciousness. With such sketchy evidence, the possibilities of an explanation which is adequate and comprehensive may always be dim.

It will be argued here that what must be understood is that the birth of consciousness and of man's language capacities, if not actual performance, must have gone hand in hand. If man's culture increased as time went by — and the record of man's artifacts shows that man's tools, his art, his skills, and his theories did grow increasingly more complex as he developed — his capacity, both mental and physical, for the use of language must have increased.

It is impossible to establish an absolute cause-and-effect priority for consciousness, language capacity, or culture. Undoubtedly at times, when first consciousness, and then culture grew more complex, language also broadened to allow for the expression of a deeper consciousness and an enriched culture. At other times when language capacity increased, greater avenues of consciousness opened and allowed for the invention, discovery and formulation of new cultural complexities. Of course, accidental invention would allow culture to have first place.

It is important to keep in mind that proto-man, although he doubtless was developing language, had little facility in applying it to convey meaning in the sense that language is used today. It is probable that proto-man's language was not much more intricate than that of his cousins the chimpanzees. J. Desmond Clark, University of California — Berkeley, states that if Middle Pleistocene man possessed language, it was doubtless at a lower level of expression than language as we know it today. The activities in which early man engaged did not require a speech "much more complex than that of Australopithecines or chimpanzees"; however, "advance can surely be postulated from the increasing brain size, as well as the learning and mastery of the stone-flaking techniques."[4] Compared to present-day language proficiency, man's early efforts at verbal communication were simple. When they are viewed from the standpoint of progress since his beginnings, the sophistication in the mind of early man was immense. Although he could signal but a few cries, his brain was already integrating information at a very high level and was no doubt already modeling or picturing the world to him in the form of symbol systems or world maps.

Modern neuropsychologists understand that the everyday world which humans experience — the world of grocery lists and household chores, the solid earth, the weather, and everyone's health — is in fact, when looked at in terms of operations in the brain, an exceedingly complex model, or, as K. J. W. Craik called it, an "explanation of reality."[5] Paleoneurologist Harry Jerison, following Craik, notes that biological intelligence is indicated by man's capacity to create a perceptual world which is a construct of the nervous system to explain to the brain incoming sensory and motor information.

Jerison discusses Craik's explanation of the role of consciousness as a conduit of reality to the brain:

> Craik's . . . description of thoughts as model building to handle the information of the senses may be the best and most complete statement of . . . the working of the nervous system. The work of vertebrate brains, beyond the level of simple reflexes, involves at least a primitive type of consciousness in which "maps" of a "real" world are created and in which an animal's behavior is developed with respect to these maps. The human animal in creating such a map also creates the real world . . . the world of everyday experience. This is the world filled with solid objects rather than the empty space that the physicists proclaim: it includes living plants and animals, more or less predictable

---

[4]"African Origins of Man the Toolmaker," in Isaac and McCown, *Human Origins*, pp. 44, 45.

[5]See K. J. W. Craik, *The Nature of Explanation* (Cambridge: Cambridge Univ. Press, 1943).

actions (which occur in similarly created "real" time) by living and non-living matter, and socially desirable and undesirable people and things.[6]

It is known then that early man used tools, that he had a simple language at least equal to the cries of chimpanzees, and that in order to gain enough control over nature to exhibit these cries, it was necessary that he possess a highly integrated neurological system. One of the hindrances in arriving at conclusions concerning the origin of language is that the study of primates is not advanced to the degree that the researcher can state definitely the amount of self-awareness actually experienced by the chimpanzee.[7]

Self-awareness involves two stages which in modern man are present together. Without doubt the first level has been achieved to a limited extent by chimpanzees and perhaps by some of the other lower animals. This level is group-oriented with an individual's experiencing integration with a larger unit in a system. In modern man this level is rarely present in isolation but is usually accompanied by more complex forms of consciousness. Situations involving the first level, however, are seen in instances of the first few minutes of waking before a person decides to go back to sleep; of a spectator caught up in watching a sports event; or of a participant in mob action. During such experiences an individual can recognize himself to the extent that he realizes that he is someone who is sleepy, or a sports fan, or a part of a mob. But he does not at that moment, and probably cannot, form an image of himself objectively as a part of ongoing logical decision or action. He does not say, "I am a person who is sleepy and is going back to sleep"; or "I am a sports fan involved in this game": or "I am a part of this mob action." Although this experience unaccompanied by other levels of consciousness is rare in man, it does exist. From what is known of chimpanzees and of early man, it

---

[6]*Evolution of the Brain and Intelligence* (New York: Academic Press, 1973), pp. 160-61.

[7]David Premack of the University of Pennsylvania surveys the limits and scope of simian intelligence in David Premack, *Intelligence in Ape and Man* (New York: Halsted Press Division of John Wiley, 1976). On the possibilities of awareness in chimpanzees, see R. Leakey and Lewin, *Origins*, p. 189.

is doubtful that their self-awareness rose above this stage. A chimpanzee can join the other members of his group in a foraging expedition and can function as a unit in the group. It is not likely that his consciousness involves an image of himself as a hunter in the expedition. The same statement can be made of early modern man. That is why early language could be limited to a simple set of cries. It is not to be supposed that words represented to early modern man what they convey to man today.

It is a flaw in biological reasoning to give much attention to the "ontogeny-recapitulates-phylogeny" view that the modern animal recapitulates in his growth from childhood to adulthood the stages which primitive organisms went through in their development. Nevertheless, it is highly probable, and it is useful as a heuristic device, to consider that in some ways the world of a modern-day infant is similar to that of early man's adulthood. It is known among psychologists that to the infant the whole of reality is himself and his undifferentiated mother. To the child of two or three, however, the world is far more complex and abstract than it had been in his earliest beginnings. He, too, has learned to separate himself, not only from his mother but from the rest of the world. He has developed a private ego and sees himself as a functioning unit separate from the universe.

The adult world of early days or that of the modern infant, the person waking up, the spectator sportsman, or the fanatic in a mob all share a tendency toward unity, toward non-differentiation of thought, toward non-reflection, toward the immediacy of the gut-level of experience. Modern man faces daily a conscious version of immediate experience which is called here the *primary* world. It can be noted that in the mind of the modern adult much of the daily routine has been taken over, as far as is possible, by unconscious or quasi-conscious modes of thinking and acting, as in the process of driving an automobile. The modern man's mind is free for more reflective thoughts during parts of the day, and some people possess high degrees of freedom from the responsibility of mundane levels. Many individuals in today's industrial world (the assembly line worker, the traditional housewife), however, have jobs and social roles which demand absorption in the quotidian, but others (artists, writers, and teachers) have more time to range beyond the immediate level of experience.

Without question the outlook of the enlightened adult of today encompasses far more than the primary world. Man's imagination is stimulated by rapidly expanding knowledge in the sciences, in technology, and in the arts, and by instantaneous exposure to world information, communication and ideology.

A key to the power of the imagination lies in the capacity, if one so chooses, to reach a second stage of self-awareness called here the world of the *secondary* imagination. This is the realm of subjective thought, the interior private world of the emotions which humans enjoy and fear. The secondary world, too, has its range of competencies. It allows, on the one hand, for the most trivial daydreams, and, in the mind of a disciplined great artist, it is, on the other hand, the source of transcendent art. It permits man to be not only a dreamer, a craftsman, or an artist. It provides him with a range of emotions and moods and the capacity to practice deceit.

Beyond the first two levels lies a *tertiary* level which involves the higher brain functions, specifically, the power of the imagination to formulate hypotheses. This level is based upon human recognition of a future, a time which has not yet happened, and also of a timeless realm of permanent truths, the home of logic and mathematics. The tertiary imagination is based upon the ability of the primary world to conjure up a level of the *now*, and the secondary world's capacity to provide a second view of the *now* which is also the *not now*, that is, a hypothetical world.

Beyond these three divisions is another, the *quarternary*, the channel of consciousness used to view the other conscious levels. The quarternary world is the source of the human's ability to see himself as a separate individual, to observe his thinking as it progresses, and to project his own thoughts as a separate entity. He is aware not only of himself as one who thinks, but, quite apart from the knowledge of his cerebral processes, he is able to recognize the very elements — the congruities and the incongruities, the pauses, and the onrushing sequences of his mentation in the context of reverie, rationalization, goals, purposes, and the like — which motivate the processes of thought.

At some stage in the development of *Homo sapiens*, the quarternary imagination allowed man to begin to see himself not only as a hunter but as a member of a hunting party. This achievement has never been reached by any other of the higher animals which hunt, such as the lion or the chimpanzee. The quarternary level is the beginning of true individualization. When it is combined with the fantasy provided by the secondary imagination, and the ability to make hypotheses from the tertiary imagination, the quarternary level eventually allows man to see himself as a subject in a universe of objects, to differentiate himself from the cosmos, to treat the world as an object, and to create systems of metaphysics, explanations of the world which reach beyond the world. With the achievement of the quarternary level, man reaches metaconsciousness. The quarternary imagination is a necessary ingredient to full consciousness.

All four levels come into play in the development of spoken language which is defined as the primary medium of communication among people. It is not the only medium. Others range from facial expression to sexual intercourse. It is not surprising that people conjecture that on another planet extraterrestial beings may be able to communicate exclusively by telepathy and not need spoken language at all. What is more, semioticians like to consider language as but another system of signs, but certain unique peculiarities of spoken human language separate human speech from other possible communication systems.

Language uses sound waves produced by the vocal apparatus for its transmission medium. It is also a linkage between brains, the communicator's and his listener's. Language has another purpose than communication. There is an inner voice, the dialogue of a person with himself.

Another layer in the language process consists of the vast, unconscious neurological processes that go into making language possible. When someone says "I feel good today," he is simultaneously reacting to his own inner make-up and offering a private statement to himself concerning his condition. He is also making a public declaration.

Language has three sources, society, the conscious individual mind, and the unconscious individual mind. Most linguists pay lip service to the contributions of the individual mind by noting that language can ultimately be divided into *idiolects,* ways in which each speaker individualizes his speech, with the total number of idiolects equaling the total number of speakers of a language. Linguists, however, treat the idiolects as deviations from the hypothetical norm of the common language.

The idiolect, made up of various elements, is the essence of conscious speech. The lexicon, primarily social, and derived from the community, is the number of words a person has at his command. Individual deviations from the lexicon are strictly forbidden by the culture. For example, an individual may decide, if he so chooses, to refer to his automobile by a nonsense phrase and call it my "nee-naw," but when he says "My nee-naw is in the shop today," no one knows what he is talking about.

Though the lexicon is assimilated from society, the individual can put it to private uses. Most persons most of the time go about opening their mouths and letting fly whatever words come to mind, but some other people — for instance, public speakers and writers — are extremely conscious of their choice of words. An analogy to the automatic nervous system may be drawn. One can allow the nervous system to do one's breathing or he can consciously force his lungs back and forth and thus can be aware of a mechanical breathing process.

Other levels of language are the phonetic, or sound system: the morphological system, which encompasses the effect of grammatical changes on words: and the syntax, the sequence of words in a sentence. All of these levels are primarily social in derivation and are used without conscious thought by many individuals.

It is, however, at the last level, the semantic, which expresses meaning, that the individual contribution becomes extremely important, although most humans cannot go as far as Lewis Carroll's Humpty-Dumpty and have their words mean precisely what the speaker wishes them to mean, nothing more and nothing less. As many wars and other catastrophes tragically testify, the same word may have radically different meaning to different people. Because of sharply divergent and even contradictory connotations of words, and because of the shades of meaning which semantics makes possible, the semantic level contributes to both the idea and its expression, adding height and breadth and depth to human thought.

# CHAPTER VII

## LANGUAGE: THE ENRICHING CAPACITY

Gradually the human began to learn to think but when an invention was stumbled upon, he did not have the capacity to make the discovery known. The news did not spread. It was perhaps not even passed on to his progeny. Today a rapid trade in communication flashes an advance in the sciences or arts immediately throughout the world. Early man had no communication network. He did not at first possess the verbal techniques for the transmission of thought. Doubtless the idea of using the same tool twice, or of feeding the offspring in a different way, would occur to an individual. Again and again, however, someone who had achieved an early sample of an exosomatic culture or an awareness of a particular patterned behavior would break through into metaconsciousness but would have to abandon the idea or procedure. He might never teach it to anyone. The new pattern would be lost.

But as individuals kept achieving new skills, gradually some parents left offspring with the capacities to maintain the earlier breakthrough. The human brain began to form more involved patterns. Competencies became more common to numbers in various groups. The potential for such culture was little by little inherited by the race through the process of natural selection. Such growth was responsible for another change.

The millions of times a tool was first used or a new recipe concocted were matched by corresponding millions of events of equal import. Someone told someone else about it. In order for such communication to take place, certain prerequisites were required. The subject-object dichotomy had to occur. Man had to cease believing that he was a homogenized part of nature and must come to understand that he was not only separated from nature, but that he lived in a world of other minds. Man had developed a secondary imagination.

Although it may be assumed that early primitive man had developed a subjective mind, it must also be noted that his mind was indeed simple. For example, consider a teaching situation involving the use of tools. A father, with his son, picks up a rock and chips away at a bone. He makes a grunt, the same sound he had made on the hunt, and encourages his son to work with him. As the son imitates his father, the boy is engaged in more than blind imitation. He is grappling with the abstract idea of tool-making, as well as the skills required of him, so that the next day he will be able to continue the work alone.

Through memory and an inherited potential for learning, the son, when he has a child, shows him the new process in material culture. Through the millenia, more humans are born with the potential to learn and to remember. At last, those individuals born without that potential are considered retarded. Meanwhile, the abilities which this potential allows grow more and more complicated. The progressive learners change more rapidly and leave more members capable of making variations in behavioral patterns and more progeny who are able to perform successfully.

A breakthrough in proto-man's journey toward the achievement of full consciousness came about a million and a half years ago when *Homo erectus* appeared.[1] Proof that *Homo erectus* had a primitive symbolic culture and a primitive subjective mind lies in his invention of fire and his application of that

---

[1] Philip Lieberman [*On the Origins of Language* (New York: Macmillan, 1975)] argues that Neanderthal men and earlier proto-humans lacked the jaw arrangement which in present-day humans allows the tongue to form the sounds of speech. His findings are contested by, among others, Marjorie Le May, "The Language Capability of Neanderthal Man," *American Journal of Physical Anthropology*, 42 (1975), 9-14. Critics argue that Lieberman's data are based on incomplete fossil skulls or on faulty analysis of his materials, and that a human child is sometimes born today with anatomical restrictions similar to those of Neanderthals and yet is able to speak. The controversy is surveyed by Peter Farb [*Humankind* (Boston: Houghton Mifflin, 1978), pp. 75-76]. Farb concludes that human speech began early but reached full flowering only with *Homo sapiens sapiens*. His findings agree with the thesis advanced here. If

invention to practical use. Fire dramatically transformed human life style. Children of earlier primitive man had learned through memory and imitation, but *Homo erectus* had a technology which altered his universe.

When one teaches a child the benefits of the use of fire, he cannot deal in primitive demonstrations accompanied by grunts. The combining of foods, or the chipping of stone makes very little difference in the ultimate condition of the material. But the process of making fire involves chemical changes in which, as if by magic, wood becomes ash, and heat and light are liberated. The use of fire, some anthropologists think, allowed man for the first time to inhabit caves. In any case, fire provided warmth, light, and a degree of safety against wild animals.

Fire is a simple technology. Man as master of fire was transforming, if only in simple ways, the material world around him. To provide warmth and light for work at night, to explain to someone that a torch can guide him through the darkness, to establish a recipe for cooking food is to harness a changing world for one's own purposes. Such new skills required an expanded language capacity in order to indicate how things change through time. The language must have forms to distinguish singular from plural. It must be structured to show relationships among words and among concepts. In order to say "The fire will protect us," or "The food will be cooked to make it more tasty," the language must have a phonology, a morphology, and a syntax.

Later, Peking man developed rituals connected with the dead. He treated death, not simply as a biological fact, but also as a hypothesis. He had a rudimentary tertiary or hypothetical

---

subsequent research were to vindicate Lieberman's position completely, the argument presented here would not be damaged since it is stated here that *speech itself* did not necessarily begin with hominids but that the *capacity for speech* began with the hominids. Lieberman himself does not challenge that claim. He states (p. 170) that the use of stone tools would suggest a cognitive development in man which calls for a transformational grammar. Robert C. Carlisle and Michael I. Siegal in rev. of *The Origins of Language* by Philip Lieberman, *American Journal of Physical Anthropology*, 47 (1977). 489-90, state that Lieberman cannot "resolve the seeming paradox between the demonstrable increase in human brain size in the course of evolution with . . . [the] presumed relative latency of the full development of human speech."

imagination. The semantics of his language was thereby enriched.

When modern man entered the scene, he had to share the stage for thousands of years, warring and intermarrying with such rivals as Neanderthal and Rhodesian man. Neanderthal man had definite funeral rituals and was well on the way to a quarternary or mythical imagination.

As modern man became the only survivor of all of his precursors, he enlarged upon his inheritance from them. His funeral ceremonials eventually became more complex with the addition of myths about the dead. His language became fully developed to encompass the richness of the quarternary world of culture.

As he is known today, modern man is truly metaconscious. Great have been his gains. He carries with him the belief that he is lord of the earth. He recognizes that he has produced impressive material culture. He is confident that he has high symbolic culture. But great have been man's losses. He has come to know that he must die. He has come to know that life, although it can be better, can also be worse. He walks with the concepts of inequality, of slavery, of back-breaking, unrewarding work for billions of people. He looks the spectre of greed and war and hunger full in the face. In his more realistic moments he tastes the bitterness both of his own ignorance and that of his fellow humans. He fears the unknown.

It is not surprising that, given a realization of his own condition and of separateness from the universe which was once his safe and certain home, he has developed key myths which are concerned with the gap between what man is and what he would be, and which consider what can be done to heal that gap. Man's mythmaking abilities constitute another facet of his conscious mind.

# PART TWO

## THE MYTHIC ACCOUNT
## OF CONSCIOUSNESS

# CHAPTER VIII

## THE DEVELOPMENT OF MYTHMAKING

After man had initiated his great cultures and had achieved a complete imagination, he began to be fully conscious. As long as he continues to exist, the levels of his awareness will continue to grow. Consciousness is an ongoing process.

As the researcher analyzes man's new abilities, it becomes difficult to be scientific because science deals with facts while the conscious mind is largely involved with a special kind of certainties. It is only at the primary level that sureties enter human thought. Most of the time facts are colored by fantasy or by hypothesis and are viewed as metaconscious quarternary concepts.

Since facts are usually not objective, it follows that it is impossible to treat them objectively. The subjects with which myths deal, however, can be considered with partial objectivity. Myths, although they are by definition concerned with non-objective facts and are always partially subjective, are also conceptualized in the quarternary level of consciousness and therefore acquire a certain objectivity as they are embodied first in language and then in texts.

Text creation is that realm of thought in which the objective and the subjective are combined in a way which highly favors the subjective but in which the objective is nevertheless always present. Text creation encompasses ideas in the writer's mind before they are incorporated into language. Traditionally, this region has been regarded as the domain of private, ephemeral fantasy, with the text, after it has been established, constituting a permanent record of a fleeting moment of creativity. This view was challenged in the 1930's by the Oxford University philologist and fantast J.R.R. Tolkien who believed that the products of human fantasy are, for individual human beings, not ephemeral, but quite real.[1] In arguing for the ontological validity of human fantasy, Tolkien questioned the traditional position, such as, for example, the views of the English romantic poet and critic Samuel Taylor Coleridge (1772—1834).

Coleridge said that the receiver of a work of literature — the reader in his chambers or the spectator at a performance — must agree for the moment to suspend disbelief and to permit the secondary mind to become the temporary possession of the author of the fiction or drama. Tolkien contends that the task of the author is rather to cause the audience to expand belief and to accept, if only for the nonce, the validity of the world of the writer. Coleridge had said that the mind has two powers, one which he called *fancy*, the ability of the mind to produce fleeting, ephemeral whimsies; and a higher power, *imagination*, which Coleridge defined as the ability of the mind to give to ideal creations the inner consistency of reality. For Tolkien the word *fancy* is deprecatory, and *imagination* is merely the ability of the mind to conjure up images. Both *fancy* and *imagination* are combined and surpassed by a third capacity of the mind which Tolkien calls *fantasy*, the ability of the mind to sub-create, to produce an art which opens up the world of the imagination. For Tolkien the second world is superior to the first one and results not only in idealistic flights but also in a literal reforming of life. He calls this world *faërie* and says of it:

> Faërie contains many things besides elves and fays, and besides dwarfs, witches, trolls, or dragons; it holds the seas, the sun, the moon, the sky, and the earth, and all things that are in it: tree and bird, water and stone, wine and bread, and ourselves, mortal men, when we are enchanted.[2]

Tolkien states that ideal creations have the inner consistency of reality because they are part of reality. The purpose of

---

[1] J. R. R. Tolkien, "On Fairy Stories," (1938), rpt. in J. R. R. Tolkien, *Tree and Leaf* (Boston: Houghton Mifflin, 1965), pp. 37, 46-47.
[2] Ibid. p. 9.

fantasy is not to mirror reality but to transform life by adding an alternate reality as a new, enriching dimension.

Robert Bellah writes that sociologists who study religion will not be able to understand the sociological impact of that subject until they have, at least for the purpose of their studies, an understanding of and an empathy with the belief system of the adherents of the religion under study. Bellah calls this system *symbolic reality* and says that the ultimate reality for humans is always symbolic, composed of symbols which reflect back upon themselves. Human beings can really, in the final analysis, know nothing more.[3]

An imagined world, however symbolic it may be, will remain the private possession of an individual unless he wishes to make it public. But any account, no matter if it is the story of a dream, a play for children, a sermon, a poem, a short story, or a novel, becomes an objective literary text if and when the artist or writer decides to present it to the public in the form of written words. Additionally, the language of art, according to the Soviet semiotician Yury Lotman, is a special kind of language of its own.[4]

A myth, however, is not only the product of the secondary imagination. It is also — and Claude Lévi-Strauss emphasizes that it is *especially* — a product of the tertiary or hypothetical imagination. Myths are always structured to give embodiment in language to private fantasy, but, owing to the nature of the human condition, myths are also efforts to solve the basic vexed problems of the uncertain circumstances in which mortals always find themselves. Myths attempt to bring harmony to eternal opposites — life and death, heaven and earth, nature and culture.

Beyond tertiary or hypothetical levels, myths are essays in the quarternary imagination. They deal in metaconsciousness. The mythmaker or the one who comes to know the myth is aware of the transcendent qualities of that which he creates or

---

[3]Robert Bellah, "Christianity and Symbolic Religion," *Journal for the Scientific Study of Religion*, 9 (1970), 92, 95.

[4]Yury M. Lotman, *Struktura khudozhestvennogo teksta* (1970): rpt. ed. Thomas G. Winner (Providence: Brown University Press, 1971), p. 16.

understands. The mythic tale itself is a component of the individual's mental world. Since myths allow man to look at himself after the fact, or paradoxically even as he is participating in the fact, it is not surprising that myth has been a favorite vehicle for man to use when he is trying to understand the phenomenon of his own consciousness.

This study deals with some of the major myths concerning consciousness which have been offered by writers in various cultures. Myths deal with hypothetical facts. It is therefore not possible to call this presentation a study in science. Instead, in order to understand myth, one must think mythically.

# CHAPTER IX

## THE SEVERED CORD: THE SEPARATION OF MIND FROM NATURE IN GREEK LITERATURE

The ancient Greeks through their mythology and their literature pondered the origin and the nature of consciousness. An instance of difference in Greek and twentieth century reaction is seen in the classic example Sophocles' *Oedipus Rex*. Followers of Sigmund Freud have viewed the play chiefly as the first literary presentation of the Oedipus complex. Certainly the incest taboo was for the Greeks one of the themes which the play explicated. The drama also involved many other subjects. Specifically, it concerned human consciousness in terms of what was for the Greek mind still a crucial question — a recent and deeply felt realization of loss of unity between man and nature.

One of the characteristics by which *Oedipus Rex* is marked from most other Greek tragedies is that, although gods are spoken of, no supernatural deity appears on stage. The absence of the physical presence of gods is compensated for by frequent references to their power, especially to that of the god Apollo who has cursed the house of Thebes.

The audience learns that the present king Oedipus had come to the throne a few years earlier by defeating a riddle posed by the sphinx. This monster's demands for tribute had impoverished the city, but during the first few years of Oedipus' reign, the people had enjoyed great prosperity, with abundant agricultural yields. Now a withering drought has blighted the Theban fields. A chorus of citizens seems to think that the source of the disaster lies somewhere in Oedipus' mind, and that he must change his relationship to the gods and to nature in order to restore the well-being of the city. The priest from the chorus says to Oedipus:

> King, you yourself
> have seen our city reeling like a wreck already . . . .
> A blight is on the fruitful plants of the earth,
> a blight is on the cattle in the fields,
> a blight is on our women that no children
> are born to them; a God that carries fire,
> a deadly pestilence is on our town,
> strikes us and spares not, and the house of Cadmus
> is emptied of its people while black Death
> grows rich in groaning and in lamentation . . . .
> Now Oedipus, Greatest in all men's eyes,
> here falling at your feet we all entreat you,
> find us some strength for rescue . . . .
> For now this land of ours
> calls you its savior since you saved it once.[1]

The chorus believes that if Oedipus could make things right again with the gods, the curse would be removed. The relationship between Oedipus' mind and the prospering of the city was probably not for Sophocles the exercise of what was later to be known as the pathetic fallacy — the belief that changes in the fortunes of men are echoed by alterations in nature and vice versa.

Rather the relationship was for Sophocles an integral part of both nature and the physical world which for the Greek mind functioned together. Lacking the modern concept of the separation both between the natural and the supernatural, and science and religion, the Greeks saw the gods as a crucial link (which was also a divider) between man and nature. The character of that link-and-divider is the key to the Greek attitude toward the separation of man and nature, the need for the healing of that separation, and the Greek account of the development of consciousness.

In classical Athens, where Sophocles wrote, the oracle of the gods was still consulted, and its commands, given through

---

[1]Sophocles, *Oedipus the King*, trans. David Grene (1942), rpt. in *The Complete Greek Tragedies*, ed. David Grene and Richmond Lattimore (Chicago: Univ. of Chicago Press, 1959), II, 11-12.

divinely inspired prophetesses, heeded. The gods conveniently spoke in equivocal terms, but the ambiguity was almost always ignored as was the fact that the gods seemed to make their pronouncements in pithy catch phrases. The Greek attitude toward the oracle's ability to prophesy was one of respect and fear. When Oedipus consults the oracle and learns that the killer of the former king must be hunted down, the chorus implores the god Apollo to speak and to spell out the city's fate:

> What is the sweet spoken word of God from the shrine of Pytho rich in gold
> that has come to glorious Thebes?
> I am stretched on the rack of doubt, and terror and trembling hold
> my heart, O Delian Healer, and I worship full of fears
> for what doom you will bring to pass, new or renewed in the
>     revolving years.
> Speak to me, immortal voice,
> child of golden Hope.[2]

The chorus respects the gods because the people believe that the gods can see, as human beings cannot, outcomes that have been predicted by fate. If someone had asked a Greek of the Golden Age why man was disunited from nature, he would probably have answered in a general way: "Fate has decreed it." Fate was all in all. The Fates were traditionally personified as three goddesses. One of the Fates wove the thread of life; the second shaped it; the third cut it. All human beings, all the gods, even Zeus, who as the great thunderer god was as close as the polytheistic Greeks came to a Judeo-Christian conception of a mighty and powerful ruler, were subjects of Fate. William Chase Greene, Harvard University classicist, explored the role of Fate in Greek literature.

> Behind . . . [Zeus] stands Moira, Fate. She guides all things: she is the moral law which Zeus violated when he laid hands on his father and thus came under the sway of the Erynes: she represents even the pattern to which the developing character of Zeus must conform; she is the law of progress, the philosophy of history in its successive stages; of her law better than the rule of Zeus may be used the term "harmony."[3]

[2] Ibid., p. 17.
[3] *Moira* (Cambridge: Harvard Univ. Press, 1944), pp. 124-25.

But whenever a discussion of fate arises, the question of free will seems destined to come up. A convention has long been held in classical studies that Oedipus was guilty of hamartia, a fatal error of judgment, that he misread his destiny, and that the tragedy unfolds as he discovers his fatal flaw. There is another theme in the play. Man is judged guilty, not only because he has done some moral or social wrong, but because he is personally impious. When the blind prophet Teiresias accuses Oedipus of parricide, Oedipus initially suspects that, in order to gain power, Teiresias is in league with Creon, the brother of Jocasta, his wife. But Teiresias answers: "Creon is no hurt to you,/but you are to yourself."[4] Sophocles hints that perhaps the plague which haunts the city and the sense of evil that is everywhere in Thebes are caused by the state of Oedipus' mind. But if the fault is in Oedipus himself, if there is evil in his life because of his presence in Thebes, if the city is not involved in this sin and might not have been cursed if Oedipus had not come there, it may be possible, Sophocles seems to speculate, that the orthodox Greek thought of the day on one point shows a basic weakness. Perhaps a philosophy of rigid determinism in which men must depend totally upon fate is invalid.

Jocasta, Oedipus' wife and mother, undaunted by the dreadful prophecy, goes so far as to challenge the Greek conception of fate itself. When Oedipus tells her that he has polluted his mother's bed, she answers:

> Why should man fear since chance is all in all
> for him, and he can clearly foreknow nothing?
> Best to live lightly, as one can, unthinkingly.
> As to your mother's marriage bed, — don't fear it.
> Before this, in dreams too, as well as oracles,
> many a man has lain with his own mother.
> But he to whom such things are nothing bears
> his life most easily.[5]

Jocasta's famous lines inspired Sigmund Freud to formulate the theses of the Oedipus complex, the presence of hidden

---

[4] Sophocles, *Oedipus the King*, II, 27.
[5] Ibid., p. 52.

desires in dreams, and dreams as representations in censored forms of suppressed thoughts. The Greeks no doubt gave at least equal attention, however, to the first lines of Jocasta's advice to Oedipus in which she denies fate, says that no one can foresee the future, and substitutes chance for the role of divinity.

Sophocles seems to indicate that fate is a necessary precondition to religion. The chorus warns Zeus that the oracle concerning the death of Laius, Oedipus' father, must be clear and true:

> No longer to the holy place,
> to the navel of the earth I'll go
> to worship, nor to Abae
> nor to Olympia,
> unless the oracles are proved to fit,
> for all men's hands to point at.
> O Zeus, if you are rightly called
> the sovereign lord, all-mastering,
> let this not escape you nor your ever-living power.
> The oracles concerning Laius
> are old and dim and men regard them not.
> Apollo is nowhere clear in honor; God's service perishes.[6]

The whole thrust of the play is that Oedipus *did* break the incest taboo. He *did* have a tragic flaw. Piety and orthodoxy are vindicated by the plot, honoring, as it were, the tradition that the drama is part of a religious festival. But Sophocles poses a philosophical question here which remains unanswered. If fate is all powerful and, at the same time, if it is the evil in Oedipus himself which pollutes the land, how could Oedipus be otherwise than that which he was fated to be?

Just as men debated in fifth century B. C. Athens whether fate exists, so do men in the twentieth century — Sophocles' question unresolved. But a second aspect of the question can now be addressed: if fate takes no part in the tangles of existence, men often blame fate for evil fortune. If fate does intervene, its workings must be evidenced in ways which lead men to think that they have free will. How does the pattern, real or imagined, work itself out?

---

[6] Ibid., pp.48-49.

The answer lies in the relationship between men and those beings who during the performance of *Oedipus Rex* were found in the same place that they always seem to be located for believers — just off stage. Those beings are the gods. When they appear in Greek tragedy, they are usually *dei ex machina* who make an entrance to help the plot along. Because they are off stage in *Oedipus Rex,* the drama has a modern flavor. Sophocles set the play in what was to the fifth century Athenian an ancient legendary time. But he was writing about tensions which concerned his contemporaries. In the Athens of his day certain groups continued to belong to mystery cults and proclaimed ecstatic mystic communion with gods. The oracle was still consulted, but the majority of fifth century Athenians were, at best, only quasi-believers in the state religion. For them the gods had fallen silent. Today many religious people consider conscience the voice of God within man. To the true believer the divine has never fallen silent but now he speaks to people only in their subjective secondary minds. Except for a few visionaries, no one claims that God to do his work appears, walks and talks in the primary world.

For the Greeks of Sophocles' day the gods had long since ceased to appear in the primary world. In the religious ecstasies of the devotees of mystery cults and in the views of some pious believers the gods still spoke to the secondary mind. But to many the gods did not speak. Sophocles links the silence of the gods to Oedipus' discovery of the evil and pollution which existed in his own mind.

The gods did not appear to men of the fifth century B.C., but, according to the literature of earlier times, the gods once walked on earth and talked to humans both face to face and by way of the human conscience. The gods as pictured in Homer, which every schoolboy read and memorized in Sophocles' day, appeared not only in the secondary imagination but as active participants in the primary world.

The man Homer, if he lived at all, probably wrote around 950-850 B.C., long before the time of Sophocles (495-406 B.C.). Whether Homer served as the principal creator or simply as the main editor of the poems which are credited to him is not a part of the literary record. It is known that a school of poets called the Homeridae, or the sons and daughters of

Homer, flourished around 900 B.C. and preserved the earliest two great poems attributed to Homer — the *Iliad* and the *Odyssey*. Since the story of the Trojan war which took place about 1250-1240 B.C. forms the plot line of the *Iliad* and the *Odyssey*, Homer, from the vantage point of fifth-century-before-Christ Athenians, was a poet who lived in the Greek High Middle Ages. He wrote about events which happened in what were the "Dark Ages" for the Athenians who went to Sophocles' plays. Homer sang of a bronze age culture which appeared after the fall of Mycenaean culture, (1400 B.C. to 1200 B.C.).

But the Greek imagination changed a great deal from the time of Homer to that of Sophocles. The relationship among men, gods and nature was much sharper in Sophocles' day than it had been in the world of which Homer wrote.

An example is seen in Book V of the *Odyssey,* Odysseus yearns to return home from the Trojan war but is forced by the gods to wander the earth. Trapped by the nymph Kalypso who makes him her lover, he spends years as a prisoner on her island. In a profound fit of depression, Odysseus is seen sitting on the shore. Zeus looks down from Olympus, decides to free Odysseus, and calls for his messenger Hermes with instructions that Hermes go to Kalypso's island and tell the goddess that it is Zeus' will that she release her captive:

> So wand in hand he paced into the air,
> shot from Pieria down, down to sea level,
> and veered to skim the swell. A gull patrolling
> between the wave crests of the desolate sea
> will dip to catch a fish, and douse his wings:
> no higher above the whitecaps Hermes flew
> until the distant island lay ahead,
> then rising shoreward from the violet ocean
> he stepped up to the cave.[7]

Kalypso receives Hermes' announcement and tells the messenger that she resents Zeus' decree that she release Odysseus. Hermes disclaims responsibility for the decision and reminds

---

[7] Homer, *The Odyssey*, trans. Robert Fitzgerald (Garden City, New York: Doubleday, 1961), pp. 94-95.

Kalypso that all the gods and goddesses are powerless against the will of Zeus:

> Zeus made me come, and not my inclination
> Who cares to cross that tract of desolation, . . .
> But it is not to be thought — and no use —
> for any god to elude the will of Zeus.[8]

The austerity of Zeus' edict that Odysseus should be set free is in contraposition to the profligate extravagance of the natural setting of Odysseus' prison and the luxurious beauty of his captor:

> Divine Kalypso,
> the mistress of the isle, was now at home.
> Upon her hearthstone a great fire blazing
> scented the farthest shores with cedar smoke
> and smoke of thyme, and singing high and low,
> in her sweet voice, before the loom a-weaving,
> she passed her golden shuttle to and fro.
> A deep wood grew outside, with summer leaves
> of alder and black poplar, pungent cypress.
> Ornate birds here rested their stretched wings —
> horned owls, falcons, cormorants — long-tongued
> beachcombing birds, and followers of the sea.
> Around the smoothwalled cave a crooking vine
> held purple clusters under ply of green;
> and four springs, burbling up near one another
> shallow and clear, took channels here and there
> through beds of violets and tender parsley.
> Even a god who found this place
> would gaze and find his heart beat with delight.[9]

Kalypso's passion for Odysseus yields to her recognition of the inevitability of obedience to the will of Zeus, and she speaks bitterly to Hermes: "But now there's no eluding Zeus's will./If this thing be ordained by him, I say/so be it, let the man strike out alone/on the vast water."[10] Later she assures Odysseus that she will give him supplies and a "following wind" to help him

---

[8] Ibid., p. 96.

[9] Ibid., p. 95.

[10] Ibid., p. 97.

reach home, but she adds somewhat ominously, "provided that the gods who rule wide heaven wish it so./Stronger than I are they in mind and power."[11]

Marked contrast is seen between the stark, solemn, abstract world of Sophocles and the melodious, multi-hued, rich milieu of Homer. A few key differences account for some of the reasons for this variance. Sophocles observed the classical unities of simplicity, and of immutability of time, place and character. Homer was writing a narrative poem in which he could range in time and place and could modify the personalities of his characters. There is also a difference in occasion. Sophocles was writing for a theater which had grown out of a religious rite. Homer was creating dramatic entertainment with heavy patriotic overtones. He needed the vast panoply of life. Finally, dissimilarity of setting in the broadest sense of the term alters focus for the two authors. Sophocles dealt with human beings at the very moment when they faced divine retribution on a temple grounds. The Athenian stage was for him a controlling symbol, not a realistic background. Homer, as Erich Auerbach has noted, was the first realist in the sense that he peopled his world with the flora and fauna of life at its fullest.[12] Underlying these contrasts is a far more vital one, a difference in psychology, an alteration of consciousness between the time of Homer and that of Sophocles which, in turn, changed the relationship between man, gods, and nature.

The constant interviews between gods and men which take place in Homer were seen in Sophocles' time as they are considered in the twentieth century. Their strength is their allegorical impact. Their weakness is that they are considered mere fantasies. No reader assumed in Sophocles' time or today that Hermes actually visited Kalypso, or that Kalypso was in fact cohabiting with a mortal, however heroic or gifted or aristocratic he may have been. The most devout believer by Sophocles' time viewed stories about gods as symbolic representation of what the believer considered a valid relationship, not a personified one.

---

[11] Ibid., p. 98.

[12] Erich Auerbach, *Mimesis* (1946), trans. Willard R. Trask (Princeton: Princeton Univ. Press, 1953), p. 13.

The devious, flamboyant, magnificent and evil activities of the gods in Homer's stories are grist today for a cinematic fantasy. Since the invention of the motion picture camera with its special effects and techniques, film directors and technicians have been able in the course of a motion picture to create such illusions that the audience in a modern version of the *Odyssey* can pretend that it is Hermes gliding over the water and that the blandishments of almost irresistible sirens must be vicariously resisted.

When the audience in Sophocles' day read Homer, they used their mind's eye to picture such a visionary world, always knowing that they were engaged in fantasy. But in Homer's day the sense of fantasy was different. The gods entered directly into the secondary imagination of Homer's audience. Men still considered their fantasies reception devices for direct messages from the gods. As Homer understood consciousness, humans shared ideas with supernatural beings. By Sophocles' time men were alone in their minds.

# CHAPTER X

## THE SEVERING SCALPEL:
## THE TRANSMUTATION OF
## CONSCIOUSNESS
## IN GREEK CULTURE

When Homer wrote centuries before our own era, modern man had emerged, and Homer had just as much access to the four areas of imagination, primary through quarternary, as creative people have in the twentieth century. Although the imagination did not change between the ninth century B. C. when Homer wrote epics and the fifth century B.C. when Sophocles produced dramatic tragedies, the Greeks' metaconscious idea of the imagination and the uses to which the Greeks put creativity had altered drastically.

The date 500 B.C., which marks the beginning of the flowering of Athens, coincides neatly with similar renaissances which took place around the same time in other cultures, for example, in the China of Confucius and in other civilizations which were turning from the worship of forms to a religion of abstractions. Historians of the development of human thought have long pondered the reason for similar changes at about the same time in three widely separated cultures where the works of each culture were almost completely unknown in the other countries.

A far-fetched answer has been offered by Princeton psychologist Julian Jaynes who proposes that a world-wide alteration in the human brain took place around 500 B. C.[1] He suggests that before this time men were not conscious in the modern sense of the term; that is, they did not possess self-awareness. While they displayed on the surface such higher

---

[1] See Julian Jaynes, *The Origin of Consciousness in the Breakdown of the Bicameral Mind* (Boston: Houghton Mifflin, 1976).

brain functions as imagination, in actual fact they lacked the central higher brain function of volition.

The rationale of Jaynes' thesis is found in psychological data well-known today. Human thought is the product of the integration of material in the two sides of the brain — the right hemisphere which is involved with the emotions and with art; and the left hemisphere which produces language and logic.

Jaynes suggests that before 500 B.C. the brain did not integrate information from the left and right sides of the brain. Instead, each side was a separate entity. The right side produced fantasies in the form of ethical and religious pronouncements and offered imaginary solutions to emotional conflicts. The left side received the material from the right side, interpreted it, and took action accordingly. The messages from the right side of the brain were the voices of the gods. Humans listened to these voices and accepted them unquestioningly. Thus people avoided the burden of consciousness and did not have to cope with self-awareness. Jaynes believes that around 500 B.C. the brain became unicameral in information processing. At that time the gods ceased to speak. The ancient voices of the gods in the bicameral mind became for modern man the still, small inner voice of conscience.

Jaynes' theory, if taken completely and literally, is, on the face of it, absurd. Not only would Homer, Amos, and Chinese philosophers who were precursors of Confucius be automatons, but the creators of literature and the architects who built the Mesopotamian ziggurats and the Egyptian pyramids would be unconscious. If, at the literal level, Jaynes' view is ridiculous, at the symbolic level it is provocative and has merit. Jaynes is correct when he says that startling changes in the metaconscious understanding of the self took place around 500 B.C. He is also accurate in his statement that the gods did fall silent about this time. Jaynes himself calls for a complete theory of paleoconsciousness, one which would account for the falling into silence of the gods.

Bruno Snell, Hamburg University classicist, who has studied the changes in the psychology of the ancient Greeks, also thinks that their psychology was radically altered between the time of Homer and that of Sophocles. Unlike Jaynes, Snell cites metaconscious changes in the understanding of mind as the reason for difference. Snell does not posit a physiological case. He sees metaconsciousness as a construct which man invented for himself. In his view, it is not that the gods ceased to speak. It is rather that men discovered that they could study consciousness. While Homer was fully conscious, he did not reflect upon the possession of the attribute of self-awareness. Homer had no conception of mind as modern man views it.

Homer had his own word for the modern term given to the judgment area of the mind. He called it *noos* (the later Greek word was *nous*). He was also aware of the emotive side of mind which he treated as a separate entity and named *thymos*, the "seat of the emotions," or "the heart" in the emotional sense of the word. A third element, the spiritual aspect of mind, also appears in Homer. It was the term for soul, *psyche*, but psyche was synonymous with animation. When a person died, his psyche poured out of him.[2]

Homer did not consider the three entities *nous*, *thymos*, and *psyche* physical objects, but they were analogous to physical organs. The analogy was valid enough so that, for all practical purposes, Homer thought that these components operated in the way that physical organs worked.[3] They had the capacity to receive stimuli from outside the body. In Homer's world the chief source of outside influence was the gods who manipulated men by affecting them in a stimulus-response manner. Thus, in Homer's metaconscious view, men were deeply influenced by the gods who, in turn, were influenced by fate. Homer considered the relationship among man, gods, and fate a constant. For him nature, gods and men were bound in close harmony. The interaction was not destined, however, to endure throughout the history of Greek culture.

The early pre-Socratic philosophers and the lyric poets around 600 B.C. offered a new version of consciousness. In lyric writings, the realization that man is a creature of fantasy emerges for the first time. Man also became metaconsciously aware of his own mortality. In literature the poet sought to reproduce those moments in which "the individual is all of a

---

[2] Bruno Snell, *Die Entdeckung des Geistes*, (1946), trans. T. G. Rosenmeyer as *The Discovery of Mind* (Cambridge: Harvard Univ. Press, 1953), p. 8.

[3] Ibid., p. 6.

sudden snatched out of the broad stream of life when he is cut off from the ever-green tree of universal growth."[4] As a result, the Greek as an individual with an ego could see himself as utterly different from the world around him. He gained recognition of his subjective mind, but in so doing he lost the belief that he was united with his universe. He became alienated from his world. The entities of the *nous*, the *thymos* and the *psyche* were no longer thought to be organs of the body. They became the personal province of the subjective mind of the poet and of his reader. The early lyric poet still maintained an absolute personal relationship with his world. It was an "I-thou" tension with the author's addressing the cosmos as "thou."

The model was short-lived. Contemporary with the early lyric poets, the pre-Socratic philosophers introduced a view of the universe as a third entity, as *it*. Fate, which for Homer had been a participatory exercise for both gods and men, became, in the tertiary hypothetical interpretation of the pre-Socratics, an abstraction, a word, a concept, an idea capable of being examined, disbelieved, and thus treated heretically.

Once again, much was gained when the universe was considered objectively. Such detachment of mind made possible philosophy, technology, and Western civilization. But much was lost. The sense of a divine link between man and the universe was gone.

Aeschylus, an immediate precursor of Sophocles, in his play *Prometheus Bound* considers both the power of fate and man's trauma in gaining mind at the cost of losing a monolithic universe. Aeschylus' protagonist, the god Prometheus, is stripped of his former power and is bound on a rock where daily his entrails are eaten by an eagle. This punishment Zeus had decreed because of Prometheus' concern for and gifts to man. After Zeus had consolidated his hold on the universe through a victorious war against the Titans, he had come to the conclusion that the race of men was expendable. His counselor Prometheus came to the aid of men:

---

[4] Ibid., p. 65.

> As soon as he [Zeus] ascended to the throne
> That was his father's, straightway he assigned
> to the several Gods their several privileges
> and portioned out the power, but to the unhappy
> breed of mankind, he gave no heed, intending
> to blot the race out and create a new.
> Against these plans none stood save I; I dared.
> I rescued men from shattering destruction
> that would have carried them to Hades' house. . . .[5]

Prometheus' gifts included fire or technology, and imagination or metaconsciousness of mind. Prometheus added another largess: "I caused mortals to cease foreseeing doom . . . . I placed in them blind hopes."[6] He admits that the be -stowal of metaconsciousness carried with it the deception that man might be immortal, but he considers this trick small price for the benefit that man had gained. His picture of the condition of man before he had received Prometheus' favors sounds like an early version of Julian Jaynes:

> [Before I gave the gift] hear what troubles there were among men: how I found them witless and gave them the use of their wits and made them masters of their minds. I will tell you this, not because I would blame men, but to explain to you the good will of my gift. For men at first had eyes but saw to no purpose: they had ears but did not hear. Like the shapes of dreams, they dragged through their long lives and handled all things in bewilderment and confusion.[7]

Prometheus, whose very name means foresight, has foreknowledge of a successor to Zeus who can overpower that ruler. Prometheus predicts that some day he himself will either have Zeus' cooperation or overthrow him. In either event, Prometheus knows that he will eventually win. Traditionally, *Prometheus Bound* has been considered the model for tragic optimism but Prometheus, however cynical he may have been in dealing with his overlord Zeus, is no philosophical heretic.

---

[5] Aeschylus, *Prometheus Bound*, (1942), trans. David Grene, rpt. *The Complete Greek Tragedies*, ed. Grene and Lattimore (Chicago, Univ. of Chicago Press, 1959), I, 319-20.

[6] Ibid., p. 320.

[7] Ibid., p. 327.

He maintains a deep respect for the Greek concept of fate. After all, it is through his knowledge of fate that Prometheus is confident that he will be free:

> Prometheus:   I must be twisted by ten thousand pains and agonies, as I now am, to escape my chains at last. Craft is far weaker than necessity.
>
> Chorus:        Who, then, is the steersman of necessity?
>
> Prometheus:   The triple-formed Fates and the remembering Furies.[8]

Aeschylus sets his play at a very early time in the mythic history of the Greeks, before the Middle Ages in which Homer wrote, and just at the time when the gods were being established. At that point, according to the myths, man was already in existence. The Greeks did not have a myth of the origins of the cosmos. It has been said that if there had been a myth of origins, Greek science and philosophy would have been impossible to formulate because they are predicated on an eternal universe. Such Greek stories as there are which touch upon creation begin with a universe, although it is a chaotic one.

Aeschylus handled communication between anthropomorphic gods and men by having the gods appear on stage. Sophocles, as has been noted, used speeches of actors and chorus to reveal actions of the gods. But philosophically, communication between mortals and gods was the same for these authors, whatever dramatic solution was offered. The relationship maintained balance between men, gods, and nature. Each entity was rigidly bound within its own province. Men were doomed to suffer and to die. The gods had no fear of mortality, but they were inexorably bound by fate. Nature was fate and could not escape its own limitations. Each of the three essences of the universe had to strike a bargain with reality. In *Prometheus Bound* Aeschylus stated that men, when they gained mind, also acquired the knowledge that they would die. At the same time, they obtained the capacity to hope. This pragmatic expression underlies Prometheus' claim that he had helped men by eliminating foreknowledge of the day of death.

---

[8] Ibid., p. 329.

Nature cannot surpass the limitations which confine its pattern. Both men and gods, when they come to know the pattern, realize that they can never read the design fully. Blindness and insight, each the other's complement, constitute the lot of both gods and men.

Aeschylus in his *Prometheus* myth uses Prometheus as the magician who explains the birth of the subject/object dichotomy. Mind is literally a gift from the gods. Through the *Prometheus* myth the Greeks sustained an emotional commitment to life. From the time of Homer through the Golden Age of Athens, the Greeks viewed the state of the dead as an existence with all of the savor of life removed. For the Greeks, Elysian Fields and the fate of humans after death lacked Elysian bliss. The plains of Hades were to them a vague realm, the home of incorporeal ghosts. The Greeks therefore lived all the more fully because they considered the final outcome of life after death a tragic prospect.

To conclude that a complete picture of Greek thought, or even of Greek literary thought, is to be found in the works of the tragedians would be false. An alternative to the fatalism of the tragedies was offered by Plato who taught that the mind is bound up with the soul, and that the soul is immortal and seeks to return to a happier, fuller state than its trapped condition in life.

Plato was working at exactly the point in time when science was to sever its relationship with mythology. His writings are as mythological as they are scientific. In the dialogue *Timaeus* Plato presents a cosmology in which the world, as far as man knows it, was created by the demiurge, a spiritual maker of heaven and earth, the fashioner of the soul and of life itself. At the end of the *Republic*, Plato and Socrates offer the myth of Er which is concerned with reincarnation. While men obviously do not lead an ideal life now, they have, at the end of life, a choice concerning what new existence they will experience in the next reincarnation. Although the decision is, in the final analysis, free, each person is strongly influenced by the way he has lived in the past. The soldier chooses to become a mighty general. The buffoon wants to return as an ape. The philosopher moves ever higher toward the ideal in each successive reincarnation.

After Plato, philosophers, for the most part, ceased to be literary men. The universe they discussed was abstract, more and more of an *it*. But Plato's literary myths and dialogues are not merely mythic stories. They are myths in the modern sense of being metaconscious explorations into the state of being alive.

Plato's view of life is profoundly optimistic. Death is not the termination of being. The soul is immortal, doomed to be born again and again, but if and when the soul chooses to move toward the ideal, the soul may eventually reach perfection.

Plato's view collides with the brutal stoicism of the tragedians, but Greek civilization was broad enough to encompass both. Neither outlook challenged the basic Greek beliefs concerning the cosmos. The Athenians put Socrates to death, not because he introduced new gods, for each time Athens entered a new city, its gods were incorporated into the Greek pantheon. Socrates was charged with introducing gods which might corrupt the young people of Athens, gods which might, by altering their view of life and of themselves in life, change their conception of consciousness.

Neither the optimism of the philosophers nor the pessimism of the tragedians disturbed the basic Greek belief that mind could be established in the universe only at the cost of the introduction of mystery. What was known came to be held in classic balance with what was unknown.

# CHAPTER XI

## THE DOUBLING OF CONSCIOUSNESS: THE JUDEO-CHRISTIAN CONCEPTION

Western culture has two sources of origin, the ancient Greeks and the Judeo-Christian tradition. The mythological explanation of consciousness which came into Western civilization from Judeo-Christian sources has its most fertile source in Jewish thought at the time (circa 100 B.C. to 100 A.D.) when Christianity branched from Judaism. The basic theme of Hebrew thought at that time was that the cosmos is only one of a cycle of universes which will endure throughout the ages. History is marked by direction and is moving rapidly toward a conclusion. God exists both outside and inside the Jewish man-divinity-nature system from which man is now partially alienated but which he will soon rejoin and strengthen. Out of this matrix the Judeo-Christian explication of consciousness was formed with roots that go far back into the beginnings of Hebrew mythology, theology and philosophy.

In both Jewish and Christian theology God is outside time and space and controls events inside time and space. He sees simultaneously all time — the past, the present and the future. According to Genesis, God created *ex nihilo* in six days the universe and the present system of time and space which humans know. At the high point of his design were man and woman whom God made rulers of the earth and set in a garden paradise where they were not to know pain or grief. But in that garden were two trees:

> And the Lord God planted a garden in Eden, in the east: and there he put the man whom he had formed. And out of the ground the Lord God made to grow every tree that is pleasant to

the sight and good for food, the tree of life also in the midst of the garden, and the tree of the knowledge of good and evil.[1]

The precise significance of the two trees has been a subject much discussed in later centuries. B.S. Childs, professor of Old Testament studies at Yale Divinity School, writes:

> The question can seriously be raised as to whether the uncertainty of the interpretation of the tree of knowledge does not stem ultimately from the fact that the author does not say precisely what he means anywhere.[2]

The traditional explication of the tree of knowledge is that its fruit gave the man and woman in the garden an understanding of the dichotomy between good and evil as well as an awareness of their own guilt in disobeying their creator. The interpretation of the meaning of the tree of life depends upon the definition of the word *life*. God gave the man and woman life when they were created, but it was not a form of immortality. Rather it was a harmonious relationship of the human with nature in his first home and with God who had put him there.

The Genesis writer uses the trees of life and of knowledge as theological symbols, but it is in the story of the expulsion from the garden of Eden that the beginnings of the Judeo-Christian conception of consciousness is found. The account of the fall of man is also a statement of the gaining of consciousness in the knowledge of good and of evil which made Adam and Eve like God:

> Now the serpent was more subtle than any other wild creature that the Lord God had made. He said to the woman, "Did God say, 'You shall not eat of any tree of the garden'?" And the woman said to the serpent, "We may eat the fruit of the trees of the garden; but God said, 'You shall not eat of the fruit of the tree which is in the midst of the garden, neither shall you touch it, lest you die.'" But the serpent said to the woman, "You shall

---

[1] Genesis 2, 8-9. All quotations from the Bible are from the Revised Standard Version (New York: Nelson, 1952). Further references are in the text.

[2] B. S. Childs, "Tree of Knowledge, Tree of Life," *The Interpreter's Dictionary of the Bible*, ed. George Arthur Buttcrick et al. (New York: Abingdon Press, 1962), IV. 696.

not die. For God knows that when you eat of it your eyes will be opened, and you will be like God, knowing good and evil."

(Gen. 3. 1-5)

Once humans had eaten of the tree of knowledge, they possessed mind. They began to think and they pondered the meaning of life and of death. Before they had tasted the fruit of the tree, they were like gods. Now they were mortal, not only because they had sinned, but because they had acquired both mind and knowledge. They had forfeited their right to live in the demi-paradise of Eden, though their new understanding of life and death gave them quasi-divinity. The next step would have been to eat of the tree of life and thus to gain immortality, but God at once took proper measures:

> Then the Lord God said, "Behold, this man has become as one of us, knowing good and evil: and now, lest he put forth his hand and take also of the tree of life, and eat, and live forever —" therefore the Lord God sent him forth from the garden of Eden, to till the ground from which he was taken. He drove out the man: and at the east of the garden of Eden he placed the cherubim, and a flaming sword which turned every way, to guard the way to the tree of life.

> (Gen. 3. 22-24)

God turns man out of the garden, and his motives are clear. He does not wish to share total divinity with man, at least not at this stage of divine plan. He also knows that man had disobeyed and hence had sinned and must be punished. Man is condemned during this cycle of history to till the fields, to earn his bread by the sweat of his brow, to bear children of the likes of Cain, to live a sinful existence, and to die.

Even at this stage of Hebraic thought, men are not treated as chattels of divinity but as potential equals and sharers with the divine in the man-divinity-nature system. In the pages of the Old Testament, written over thousands of years, a history of a chosen people, the Jews, and their plight is told. But there is a theme latent in the earliest chapters of the Bible that the fall of man is only the first episode in a divine drama, that out of the seed of the people of Israel will come salvation, to the Jew first, but also to the Gentile.

As Christianity developed, the Jewish concept of life as a part of sacred history had become far more complex and sophisticated than it had been at the writing of Genesis. A rigid conclusion to divine history was now envisioned. Escatology, the study of the terminus of history, can in Jewish religion be traced to 1800 B.C., reaching its culmination around the time that Christianity branched from Judaism.[3]

In early Hebrew theology God was considered a tribal deity; Hebrew salvation would come as part of tribal purification. Subsequently, the Jews began to consider the concept of a holy abode, a place for the dead called Sheol. Gradually salvation came to be considered a matter for the individual rather than for the people as a whole. About 100 B.C. a group of apocalyptic writings appeared, but apocalypse, a Greek term for revelation, was in Jewish writ concerned with the end of divine history. The chief Old Testament apocalyptic representative is the Book of Daniel in which the prophet tells of his vision:

> As I looked
> thrones were placed
> and one that was ancient of days took
>     his seat:
> his raiment was white as snow,
> and the hair of his head like pure
>     wool:
> his throne was fiery flames,
>     its wheels were burning fire.
> A stream of fire issued
>     and came forth from before him:
> a thousand thousand served him,
> and ten thousand times ten thousand
>     stood before him:
> the court sat in judgment,
>     and the books were opened.

(Dan. 7. 9-12)

Daniel describes Satan, who appears in the vision as a huge-clawed beast, and the onset of the everlasting kingdom. One of those who stood by the throne tells Daniel:

[3]An older but a valuable treatment of eschatology is R. H. Charles, *A Critical History of the Doctrine of a Future Life in Israel, in Judaism, and in Christianity* (1899; 2nd ed., 1913; paperback rpt. as *Eschatology* (New York: Schocken Books, 1963).

> And the kingdom and the dominion
> 　and the greatness of the kingdoms
> 　　under the whole heaven
> 　shall be given to the people of the
> 　　saints of the Most High;
> their kingdom shall be an everlasting
> 　　kingdom,
> 　and all dominions shall serve and
> 　　obey them.

(Dan. 7.27)

The Book of Daniel contains a central dogma of the terminus of history, a time which will usher in a resurrection of the body, an intermediate period when all will be kept in a state between the realms of the living and the dead, and a final stage when all people will either be annihilated or sent to an eternal abode which will be a place of great happiness or of great sorrow. The apocalyptic promise defines a different level in the development of consciousness, and different people will experience the new state variously. According to some apocalyptic writers, the consciousness of some of the dead will be totally obliterated, but, in most writings, some will have a future consciousness of utter pain, whereas others will experience divine consciousness.

Jewish millenial themes in such documents as the Book of Daniel found their way into the New Testament, especially in the Revelations of John the Divine. John speaks alternately of the dreadful fate of the damned and the blissful destiny of the saved, but a more paradoxical escatology is represented in the teachings of Jesus.

Jesus makes many allusions to the end of divine history, references as literal and as brutal as those espoused by John, but Jesus is also interested in the present state of human beings. He presents a novel form of consciousness which is partially available to believers now and which will be completely offered to men after his second coming. According to Writ, the explication of consciousness advanced by Jesus is based on the belief that God through Jesus is the single author of life:

All things were made through him, and without him was not anything made that was made. In him was life, and the life was the light of men. . . . and the word became flesh and dwelt among us.

(John 1. 1-4; 14 )

The author of the Gospel of John signals, however, that with Jesus' teachings a new conception of life and a new chance to become primary and divine offspring of the deity are opened:

But to all who received him, who believed in his name, he gave power to become children of God; who were born, not of blood nor of the will of the flesh nor of the will of man, but of God.

(John 1. 12-13).

Jesus says that God wishes salvation for all and has sent his Son to extend it. Those who do not take advantage of the offer of life shall meet with the most rigid future damnation. Jesus states that the believer can, however, avoid the time of judgment and go directly to eternal life:

Truly, truly, I say to you, he who hears my word and believes him who has sent me, has eternal life; he does not come into judgment, but has passed from death to life.

(John 5.24)

Belief in Jesus not only assures freedom from pain and certainty of bliss in the future forever, but acceptance is also present gain. It is a restoration in the context of this life of the divine vision which was lost at the fall of man in the garden of Eden. Jesus stated that the kingdom of God is within every person. Here an attempt is made to teach that the Christian experiences consciousness on two levels. With double vision he can live in this world with its pain and confusion while at the same time he can see the coming kingdom of God.

The twentieth-century existentialist German Protestant theologian Rudolf Bultmann centered his emphasis around the double vision theme in Christianity. The Christian, Bultmann reasons, will escape death through participation in eternity.[4] Life in eternity begins, not on judgment day, but

---

[4] See Rudolf Bultmann, *The Presence of Eternity* (New York: Harpers, 1957), p. 152.

now. This existential eternal present occurs simultaneously with chronological time for the Christian who lives in both the area of his secondary private thoughts and in the metaconscious vision which he constructs for his life. He is able in a dead and dying world to accept the reality of day-to -day living and to know the validity which Jesus gave to one of the two thieves crucified with him: "Today you shall be with me in paradise."(Luke 23. 42).

The Judeo-Christian element in Western culture, when united with the Greek strain in the tradition, produced a curious hybrid. Consciousness for the ancient Greek had been a part of the harmony and balance with the universe which was gained at the inevitable price of ignorance about the ultimate nature of that universe. Although the Judeo-Christian position held that consciousness was a treasure stolen from God, for the true believer it was also a gift returned from God to man. The merging of the two traditions in Western thought produced the quaint theory of consciousness which reigned in Europe from the time of the church fathers until the close of the Middle Ages. Man was seen as a creature capable of understanding in an extremely limited way the divinity of the universe. He was also an unrepentant sinner who through his very act of gaining consciousness had dared to defy God. The mysterious world which the ancient Greeks had found so poignant and beautiful was now a dark covering, at times masking and at times revealing the might of a wrathful deity. Nevertheless many an humble Christian in the Middle Ages became reconciled to the grimness of his world and lived his life cheerfully, believing that while he was suffering on earth, he was already a partial citizen of heaven.

# CHAPTER XII

## THE MIND AND SUPERNATURE
## IN THE WEST

In the Middle Ages mind, life, and consciousness were ethical terms. The pilgrim on earth possessed mind which was his access to the laws of God. But his consciousness, tainted by original sin, was a battleground between God and the devil. The words *consciousness* and *mind* in the literary myths of the day did not appear as isolated concepts or as abstractions. Writers allegorically demonstrated consciousness in concrete terms by showing it in operation.

An example of the medieval view is seen in the "Pardoner's Tale" from Chaucer's *Canterbury Tales*. The story is set in a time of plague. Three drunken rowdies, hearing that death is going about killing people, vow to go out and kill death himself. On their way to find death, they meet an old man and threateningly demand that he tell them where death is. At first the old man demurs, but at length answers:

> "Now, sires," quod he, "if that yow be so leef
> To fynde Deeth, turne up that croked wey,
> For in that grove, I lafte hym, by my fey.
> Under a tree, and there he wole abyde;
> Nought for youre boost he wole hym no thyng hyde
> Se ye that ook? Right there ye shal hym fynde
> God save yow, that boghte agayn mankinde
> And yow amende!" Thus seyde this olde man . . .[1]

---

[1] Geoffrey Chaucer, "The Pardoner's Tale," *The Canterbury Tales* in *Works*, ed. F.N. Robinson (1933: Boston: Houghton Mifflin, 1957), p. 153.

In a Modern English prose translation, the account reads:

> "Now, sirs," the old man answered, "if you are
> so eager to find Death, turn up this crooked path;
> for I have left him in that wood, by my faith, under a
> tree. He will stay there. He won't conceal himself
> from you because of your boasting. You see that oak?
> You shall find him right there. May God who redeemed
> mankind save and amend you." The old man spoke thus . . . .[2]

Indeed these ne'er-do-wells do not need to look farther. They have found death. Under an oak tree where the old man said that death would be waiting, they discover a treasure. Deciding that they do not have enough energy to cart all the gold back to town, they draw straws to decide which one is to return for victuals. While one is gone, the other two plot his death and upon his return kill him.

But their victim had purchased from an apothecary poison which he had put into the wine which the two murderers drink. They, too, go to their graves.

Death for Chaucer is a phenomenon realized in the primary area of consciousness. It is an abstraction which forever becomes concrete. It is disease and plague. Allegorically it is avarice and murder. It also has a location in the secondary private world of men's minds, but that area is as rigidly bound by sin and death as is the primary world. Within the stark limits of life as a brief rite of passage to an everlasting fate, the idea of mind, when it was considered at all, was viewed within the medieval framework as a functioning aspect of the general order of things, so normal that it was given no special place or notice.

Medieval man accepted a whole panoply of witches, ghosts, fairies and fiends and considered them as real as were humans. Tragic proof of such literal belief is found in the witchcraft trials and the burnings at the stake of thousands of innocent victims, a custom which persisted into early modern times. In the Middle Ages shadowy phantoms were seen as a part of the primary world and were not held to be exceptions to the natural

---

[2] *The Canterbury Tales*, trans. Ralph Lumiansky (New York: Simon and Schuster, 1948), p. 234.

order. Belief in these non-worldly creatures did not give a person the label of being superstitious. In modern times a complete reversal on this question has for the most part occurred.

With the Renaissance neo-Platonists, philosophical explications that mind is a free agent trapped in the material world again gained credence. The early modern philosophers, however, had to adjust to a view of the cosmos sparked first by Copernicus and Galileo, and later by Sir Isaac Newton. In the new physics and astronomy, the world was a machine, and the concept of mind had to be shifted out of the system of nature to become a part of the realm of the supernatural. The rationalism of Descartes and later of the Occasionalists in the seventeenth and eighteenth centuries represented the repudiation of the mechanistic view. Mind was now represented as a separate realm from the natural order and became an aspect of the natural scene during human thought only by the intervention of an omnipotent God.

The climate of opinion which was to turn mind into a supernatural entity was reflected in the literary mythology of early modern times. Consciousness came to be linked to such preternatural power as the telepathic, the clairvoyant, and the phantasmagorical. In the wake of the Newtonian mechanistic model of the universe, magic became even less a part of nature and was seen as a part of the world of the beyond.

The shift in the relationship of mind and matter can be seen in a comparison of William Shakespeare's attitude toward the supernatural with that of Chaucer. In Chaucer the world was all of one piece. All other realms were like the primary world. The secondary area of private human consciousness could communicate with the divine order. The ruling tertiary hypothesis postulated a Christian commonwealth and a future judgment day and beyond. The mind was a natural part of the cosmos.

A different attitude informs Shakespeare's *Hamlet*. Whatever may have been Shakespeare's personal philosophy concerning the possibility of the return of the dead, his character Hamlet was definitely a believer. Hamlet may be seen as a man feigning madness, or as one who is mad, or as one who is, at a deeper level, profoundly sane. Hamlet sees his own dilemma as a superstitious fear of death and asks what man would be willing to endure the heavy burden of consciousness:

> To grunt and sweat under a weary life,
> But that the dread of something after death,
> That undiscovered country from whose bourn
> No traveler returns, puzzles the will,
> And makes us rather bear those ills we have
> Than fly to others that we know not of?
> Thus conscience does make cowards of us all...[3]

Hamlet had good reason to wonder what happens to mortals in the world of the dead since he had recently entertained a visitor from beyond the grave — his father's ghost. The specter describes the other world cryptically but in such a way as to give Hamlet a thorough fright concerning the condition of the dead and his own future in that unknown state. The ghost of Hamlet's father tells him:

> I am thy father's spirit
> Doomed for a certain term to walk the night
> And for the day confined to fast in fires,
> Till the foul crimes done in my days of nature
> Are burnt and purged away. But that I am forbid
> To tell the secrets of my prison house,
> I could a tale unfold whose lightest word
> Would harrow up thy soul, freeze thy young blood,
> Make thy two eyes, like stars, start from their spheres,
> Thy knotted and combined locks to part
> And each particular hair to stand on end
> Like quills upon the fretful porpentine.
> But this eternal blazen must not be
> To ears of flesh and blood. . . .

(Act I, Scene 5, p.894)

The presence of a ghost in *Hamlet* is not unusual. Ghosts were a part of the Elizabethan stage material and were especially popular in revenge plays such as *Hamlet*. Shakespeare

---

[3] *The Tragedy of Hamlet, Prince of Denmark*, III, i, rpt. in William Shakespeare, *Shakespeare: The Complete Works*, ed. G.B. Harrison (New York: Harcourt, Brace & World, 1952), p. 906. Further references are in the text and give the act and scene number of *Hamlet* and the page number of the Harrison edition.

was, however, perfectly capable of voicing at the proper time a cynical attitude toward the supernatural. In the first part of *Henry IV*, the Earl of Northumberland, Henry Percy, nicknamed Hotspur, mocks the Welsh chieftain Owen Glendower. When Glendower claims, "I can call spirits from the vasty deep," Hotspur chides, "Why, so can I, or so can any man;but will they come when you do call for them?"[4] Although at times Shakespeare is cynical about the possible appearance of supernatural apparitions, in other moods he seems to take them seriously and to consider such manifestations tokens of the vastness of the universe and of the potentials in the scheme of things. When Hamlet tells his friend Horatio about the ghost's message, Horatio, who has himself seen the ghost, is surprised at the unearthly caller's challenge and at the very fact that he has appeared and spoken. Hamlet asks Horatio and Marcellus to swear on his sword that they will not reveal the secret of the visitation, and the ghost himself adjures them to swear to keep silent. When Horatio shudders and cries out, "Oh, day and night, but this is wondrous strange," Hamlet immediately reassures him:

> And therefore as a stranger give it welcome. There are more things in heaven and earth, Horatio, Than are dreamt of in your philosophy.
>
> (Act I, Scene 5, p. 896)

Some critics like to ponder whether Shakespeare himself was closer to the scoffing Hotspur or the believing Hamlet. In the final analysis, the personal Shakespeare exhibits those ambiguities toward the marvels of the world that many other men since early modern times have evidenced. He may well have been like others in his day and in ours — a part-time believer. He may have given more credence to ghosts while walking alone at night on a dark London street than when laughing about it later with friends in the Mermaid Tavern on a cheery autumn afternoon.

Robert H. West, who has made a thorough study of Shakespeare's belief in the supernatural, states that "Shake-

---

[4] *The First Part of King Henry the Fourth*, III, i, rpt: in Shakespeare, *Shakespeare: The Complete Works*, ed. G. B. Harrison, p.635.

speare shows . . . a reserve on the supernatural that seems akin to the reserve he shows about most things that touch on ultimate questions. He simply does not make many ultimate assertions in his plays."[5] West adds:

> In our time supernature hardly seems a valid concept even to those thinkers concerned with what used to be considered its phenomena. One has to read only a little in *The Journal of Parapsychology* and kindred organs to understand that what were once supernatural phenomena are now naturalized, and he may read even less in contemporary theology to realize that divine supernature now hardly assumes a local habitation or makes practical response to worshippers, or is, in fact, personal in any easily imaginable sense. In Jacobean times, though, when the supernatural was traditionally just above the moon and God himself answered prayers with practical gifts of healing, protection, and retribution, the direct experience of outer powers was, though not ordinary, yet generally acknowledged and even expected.[6]

Shakespeare may have conformed to the tenets of the Middle Ages in that ghosts appear in his works as they did in medieval lore. Shakespeare differs from the prevailing philosophy of the Middle Ages in the way he approaches the question of belief in spirits. The ghost of Hamlet's father appears on the battlements, but his chief field of operation is in the mind of Hamlet. Nothing is, Shakespeare thought, but thinking makes it so. The ghost of his father is the spur which drives Hamlet to revenge. He changes Hamlet's mind-set. He is a supernatural agent working through what was for Shakespeare a metaphysical instrument, an entity beyond nature — human consciousness. It is the mind, reasons Hamlet, that makes man such a piece of work and causes him to be like a god.

Another function of the apparition in *Hamlet* is that its appearance allowed the playwright to say that death itself could cross temporarily back into life. The exchange of roles of

---

[5] Robert H. West, *Shakespeare and the Outer Mystery* (Lexington: Univ. of Kentucky Press, 1968), p. 55.
[6] Ibid., p. 53.

life and death represents a new conception of the subject-object dichotomy. Although some believers could see God as a totally supernatural being, others were coming to conceive of a deity functioning behind nature but divorced from nature itself. Nature was no longer interpreted as the natural way God worked on the human scene. With the disappearance of the belief in a God who was a direct participant in the man-divinity-nature concept, another system, man-nature-supernature, came into being. The essence of the concept of supernature was now the human being, and, more particularly, the human mind.

The eighteenth century was marked by an age of deism in theology; a Newtonian view in the physical sciences; and a neo-classical humanism in the social sciences and in the arts. "The proper study of mankind," said Alexander Pope, "is man." Belief in the supernatural came to be considered unenlightened and the grossest of superstitions. The neo-classicists, however, were faced with many enigmas which they could not explain — the reasons why enlightened man continued to be a creature of capricious emotion; the formulation of an atomic theory of matter; and experiments in electricity carried out by such men as Benjamin Franklin and in hypnosis pioneered by Mesmer. These discoveries were treated by materialists, however, as mysteries which later would be cleared up when incorporated into the mechanical world picture. James Clerk Maxwell did provide a mechanistic account of electricity in the last half of the nineteenth century. Hypnotism remains only partly explained.

During the nineteenth century, metaphysicians such as Hegel insisted upon an ultimate incorporeal plane of the spirit underlying the apparent mechanism of the physical world, but philosophers of the time treated mind as an essence divorced from the mechanical system. Meanwhile, scientists of a mechanistic bent continued to press the case for a physical account of mind. These attempts reached something of a climax in the latter part of the nineteenth century when the biologist Thomas Henry Huxley proposed that mind is only an epiphenomenon, a secondary by-product of molecular action in the brain upon which mental life is totally dependent.

A reaction against the mechanistic view was represented by

the advocates of *Naturphilosophie*[7] who, during the eighteenth and nineteenth centuries, presented a vitalistic, organic interpretation of nature. If it lacked a science, the counter-movement was rich in literary mythology. Especially persuasive and powerful were a group which loosely centered around Goethe. Yet *Naturphilosophie* and similar lesser vitalistic thinking that informed, for example, Shelley of *Prometheus Unbound,* whatever the scientific pretensions of the proponents, had no scientific base. Because the vitalists were literary men, scientists came to reject vitalism and the organic theories on which vitalism was based. But to the advocates of an organic nature, mind remained a quickening, supernatural entity, not a part of the normal order. It took a revised science in the twentieth century to give a new life, although not a vitalistic breath, to the organic view of nature. Scientists did not yield an inch in their insistence upon the validity of the mechanistic model, but their view of the meaning of *mechanism* and the scope which it encompassed radically changed.

Although Darwin's introduction of the possibilities of a quasi-mechanical view of the development of life had again inscribed consciousness as a part of nature, discoveries in physics in the early twentieth century indicated that nature herself behaved at times in ways that would earlier have been described as supernatural. The theory was advanced that mind might be an essential component of matter in the physical world and that matter might appear in structures both harmonious and contradictory. In attempting to cope with the new version of nature offered by Einstein and the quantum physicists, philosophical theorists came to realize that the system of man-nature-supernature would have to be rewritten once again. With the end of the snobbery which had been a part of colonialism in the nineteenth century, Western thinkers began to look with new respect at non-Western explications of consciousness to which the radically new physics was hospitable. One such explanation was offered by the Buddhists.

---

[7] For the ramifications of *Naturphilosophie* in German literature see Alexander G. F. Gode-von Aesch, *Natural Science in German Romanticism* (New York: Columbia Univ. Press, 1941).

# CHAPTER XIII

## JAPANESE BUDDHIST DRAMA: LIFE, DEATH AND BEAUTY

For the Buddhist an explication of consciousness and of the levels of self-awareness is paradoxical. Understanding comes only to those who share experience, but enlightenment by definition is solitary — a disciplined transcendence achieved by one individual. After the Buddha, christened Guatama, had fulfilled prophecy by seeing in the same day an old man, a sick man, and a corpse, he renounced the world. As he sat under a bo-tree, caught within the limited and incomplete self he had inherited from nature, he wrestled with the natural desires which were prohibiting his attainment of a state of selflessness until he had achieved enlightenment.

Later he did not prescribe a rigid pattern through which his followers could emulate him. He did not say that his experience was in any way supernatural. Having worked out a heightened awareness privately within his own mind, he spoke little concerning it.

Buddhists have often been accused by investigators in the West of being agnostic. Certainly nothing in the teachings of the Buddha necessitates belief in a personal deity. During Guatama's lifetime, he would never answer four questions: whether the universe is eternal; whether it is finite; whether life is the same as the body; and whether when an individual achieves enlightenment, he also gains life after death. Such mysteries are meaningless after one has reached a state of being termed nirvana, a radical change of outlook, a blanketing of the thought processes in order that one can be free of desire, an explosion in which the mind empties itself of all that it had previously been and known. To the Buddha, desire is the cause of evil. Having experienced nirvana, one comes to know that all that is not enlightenment is pain. Life is pain. Birth is pain. Death is pain. Enlightenment is the absence of pain. Guatama believed in reincarnation, a doctrine of Hinduism, the religion Guatama had known since childhood. He adopted from Hinduism the concept of the vicious circle called *samsara*, the round of birth and death, and of *karma* which shapes the individual in his successive lives. The enlightened one can gain deliverance from life, death, and rebirth when he attains nirvana. Desire, the source of pain, is replaced by emptiness. The antitheses, birth and death, pain and delight, cause and effect, are equally without significance and value.

After Guatama's death, a number of changes were incorporated into Buddhism.[1] Enlightenment as practiced by the Buddha is a very difficult state, and many Buddhists say that only Guatama completely attained it. Many sects of Buddhists have contributed additions to the Buddha's teachings by which they propose to simplify and to make the way to nirvana more understandable.

Zen-Buddhists believe that one can achieve enlightenment psychologically. One can reach satori, the Zen-Buddhists' word for nirvana, by changing the very cognitive processes radically, by splitting the mind into two parts, and by living mentally the basic contradictions of life at the same time. When one realizes that he can be in two places and in two periods of time simultaneously, the mind will be wenched violently out of its former channels and will literally be exploded. Zen-Buddhists' teachings are often in the form of koans or riddles which sound as if they might have come from *Alice in Wonderland:*
The following koans are illustrative:

> Buddha told a parable in a sutra:
>
> A man traveling across a field encountered a tiger. He fled, the tiger after him. Coming to a precipice, he caught hold of the root of a wild vine and swung himself down over the edge. The tiger sniffed at him from above. Trembling, the man looked down to where, far below, another tiger awaited below to eat him. Only one vine sustained him.

[1] Two general surveys of Buddhism are Edward Conze, *Buddhism*, 3rd ed. (1951: New York: Harper, 1959) and R. H. Robinson, *The Buddhist Religion* (Belmont, Cal.: Dickenson Publishing Co., 1970).

Two mice, one white and one black, started to gnaw away at the vine. The man saw a luscious strawberry near him. Grasping the vine with one hand, he plucked the strawberry with the other. How sweet it tasted![2]

> Meeting a Zen master on the road,
> Face him neither with words or silence.
> Give him an uppercut
> And you will be called one who understands Zen.[3]
>
> Daibai asked Baso: "What is Buddha?"
> Baso said: "This mind is Buddha."[4]
>
> A monk asked Baso: "What is Buddha?"
> Baso said: "This mind is not Buddha."[5]

To one who has achieved satori, it becomes obvious that in a mad universe the very desire for life must be avoided. Rather one should savor the sweet berries of enlightenment. The instructions to knock the Zen master down in order to prove to one and all that the attacker "understands Zen" aptly demonstrates that enlightenment is a shocking truth. The graphic body-punch metaphor is that the truth of enlightenment hits one like a ton of bricks. There is method in Zen's madness. The contradictory explanations of Baso to the monk and to Daibai serve to show that it is impossible to give an adequate explanation of the role of the Buddha, and that enlightenment which the Buddha represents is beyond all activities of the cognitive processes.

The Amidists, the other Buddhist cult of interest here, are far less concerned with difficulties encountered in achieving satori. They see the Buddha as a timeless ideal element called *amida*, "the Lord of Boundless Light," and believe in a paradise where the souls of the faithful go. Their response differs from Guatama's refusal to answer questions about life and death. While Guatama taught that enlightened souls escape the wheel of continued existences, the Amidists believe that the dead

---

[2]Paul Reps, ed. *Zen Flesh, Zen Bones: A Collection of Zen and Pre-Zen Writings* (Rutland, Vermont and Tokyo: Charles E. Tuttle Co., 1957). pp. 38-39.
[3]Ibid., p. 149.
[4]Ibid., p. 144.
[5]Ibid., p. 147.

who have not yet completely reached enlightenment must rid themselves of whatever desire for life they still possess. They must return to earth as spirits until they cease to desire life.

If the teachings of Buddha can be translated into the terminology of consciousness used here, it may be said that the Buddhists realize that, while permanent alteration of the primary world is impossible, one can radically change one's personal secondary imagination and cease to make tertiary hypotheses involved with cause and effect. Thus by means of the quarternary or mythic imagination one reaches full metaconsciousness.

Just as Christian scriptures, with the exception of several statements in Revelations about streets of gold, have few references to conditions in heaven other than assurances that heaven is a state of bliss, so Buddhists' writings contain little about the mind of one who has reached enlightenment. Guatama seemed to indicate that the order of reality in which cause and effect function has always been and will always be here. Some humans will be able to rid themselves of *samsara,* the burden of the round of birth and death. The best that most people can hope for is that, while they are in a stage of transition, they can live in two worlds at the same time. Though they find themselves in a linear cause-and-effect milieu, they can also attempt to experience nirvana. It is out of the predicament of those attempting to reach enlightenment that the mythology of consciousness appears in literature inspired by Buddhism.

Especially perceptive examples of the plight of those seeking enlightenment occur in the Nō dramas (Nō means performance or talent exhibition). Beginning in the twelfth century in Japan, these dramas are presented in that country today. The basic plot line is the belief that the souls of those who do not gain complete enlightenment while on this earth must return after death in the form of ghosts. The narrative sequences of Nō dramas are often concerned with legends which usually involve some noteworthy person: a famous soldier, a statesman, a beautiful woman, a governor, or someone who has endowed a shrine or who has had some celebrated geographical entity named for him.

The famous person, who becomes the principal character in the play, is shown returning to earth after death. The drama, always performed in one act without intermission, consists of conversations between the protagonist and a living relative or colleague. The orchestra, present on stage, is small and is made up of oriental instruments. As in ancient Greek drama, few actors appear. There is a chorus which does not participate directly in the action but sits on stage and chants. It provides background information and commentary, and at times speaks for one or another of the characters. Both male and female roles are played by men who wear rich, intricately embroidered robes and masks. The dialogues are accompanied by slow, elaborate dancelike motions. They are half-sung. Thus the Nō dramas have elements of what in the West would be ballets or operas. The inflections of the speeches are not subtle. Loud tones indicate anger, soft ones, sadness. With so little scenery and other stage effects, the words of the playwright assume particular importance.[6]

The dramas of two of the most distinguished writers in the Nō tradition, Kan'ami Kiyotsugu (1333-1384) and his son, Zeami Motokiyo (1368-1443), are Amidist in form and Zen in philosophy.[7] The central thesis is Amidist — ghosts, having returned to earth, still love the beauties and the pleasures of life and do not want to give them up. The Zen elements are present because Zen has traditionally been the religion of artists in Japan. No humor or quaint Zen riddles, no jokes or pithy nonsense inform the Nō drama. A much more serious Zen concept is at work. The nearness to enlightenment in the crevices of a mind blown apart flavors the presentation. The characters speak in beautiful poetry and prose-poetry. In Zeami's play *Obasute*, for example, an aged crone, the ghost of an old woman, longs for life:

---

[6]Brief introductions to the Nō theatre are found in Faubion Bowers, *Japanese Theatre* (New York: Hermitage House, 1952), pp. 13-26 and P. G. O'Neill, *A Guide to Nō* (Tokyo and Kyoto: Hinoki Shoten, 1953), pp. 1-13. A longer treatment is Donald Keene, *Nō: The Classic Theatre of Japan* (1966: paperback ed. rpt. Tokyo: Kodansha International, Ltd. and New York: Harper & Row, 1973).

[7]On the mixture of Amidist and Zen elements in the Nō drama see Arthur Waley, trans. and ed. *The Nō Plays of Japan* (1922: paperback ed. rpt. New York: Grove Press, 1957), pp. 57-59.

Chorus:              Like the lady-flower nipped by time,
(speaking for        The lady-flower past its season.
the ghost)           I wither in robes of grass;
                     Trying to forget that long ago
                     I was cast aside, abandoned,
                     I have come to Mount Obasute.
                     How it shames me now to show my face
                     In the [mountain called] Sarashina's moon-
                         light,
                     Ah, well, this world is all a dream —
                     Best I speak not, think not,
                     But in these grasses of remembrance
                     Delight in the flowers. . . .[8]

These sentiments echo a major theme of the Nō plays: one must forsake the fragile beauty of life in order to achieve enlightenment. The returned spirit does not wish to leave the delights once known. Unlike ghosts in the tradition of the Western world who are forced to return to earth to atone for past misdeeds in order to rid their minds of disquietude, the shadowy heroes and heroines of Nō dramas love the world. Zeami and Kan'ami have altered the system of man-deity-nature which becomes man-life-beauty.

Five plays in the Nō repertory deal with the princess Ono No Komachi. She was not only of royal blood but a gifted poetess and a great beauty who lived at the Henan court during the ninth century. After her death she was the subject of many biographies although few facts concerning her are known. Much of what has been written is legend.

It is said that Komachi had a lover named Captain Fukakusa. Time after time she refused to yield to him, but at last she made a bench from the shaft used to support the wheels of her carriage and told him that he was to sleep on the bench for one hundred nights and make a bench mark each night. At the end of that time, she would give herself to him.

On the hundredth night the captain's father dies. Komachi sends the captain a mocking poem, offering to make the hundredth mark herself.[9] In Zeami's play *Komachi at Sekidera*

[8]Zeami, *Obasute*, trans. Stanleigh H. Jones, Jr., as *The Deserted Crone* in Donald Keene, ed. *Twenty Plays of the Nō Theatre* (New York: Columbia Univ. Press, 1970), pp. 124-25.
[9]Keene, *Twenty Plays of the Nō Theatre*, p. 52.

*(Sekidera Komachi)* an abbot brings children on a festival day to a religious retreat at Sekidera where he finds Komachi, now an old woman, living alone in a hut.[10] The abbot is observing the time-honored ceremonial at Tanabata, a day of poets and lovers. In ancient Japanese astronomy the seventh night of the seventh month is the only time of the year when the cowherd star can cross the river of heaven to court the weavergirl star. In observance of the lovers, bamboo branches are decorated with colored streamers on which are written poems to commemorate that romantic rendezvous.[11]

The abbot asks Komachi the secret of poetry and she answers: "Just remember this: if you will make your heart the seed, and your words the blossoms, if you will steep yourself in the fragrance of the art, you will not fail to accomplish true poetry."[12]

But Komachi has lost her beauty and is old and dying. Her life has become sad. The Komachi on the stage quotes a poem by the historical Komachi (Number 850 of the collection Shinkokinshū):[13]

> "The living go on dying
> The dead increase in number,
> Left in this world, ah —
> How long must I go on
> Lamenting for the dead?"
> 
> (p. 73)

The fictional Komachi's thoughts are voiced by the chorus:

The old
woman:              "The temple bell at Sekidera
(Chorus:            Tolls the vanity of all creation.
speaking            To ancient ears a needless lesson.
for her)            A mountain wind blows down Ōsaka's slope
                    To moan the certainty of death.

---

[10] Ibid., p. 67.

[11] Ibid., pp. 66-67, p. 78, n.l.

[12] Zeami, *Sekidera Komachi*, trans. Karen Brazell as *Komachi at Sekidera* in Keene, *Twenty Plays of the Nō Theatre*, pp. 70-71. Further references are in the text and give the page number of the Brazell translation.

[13] Keene, *Twenty Plays of the Nō Theatre*, p. 79, n. 19.

Its message still eludes me. . . .
Still in this hut I find my pleasure. . . ."

(p. 74)

Absorbed in the beauty of her life and art, Komachi continues to write poetry and to savor her own thoughts and experiences in this world. Yet realistically she knows that life for her is vain and useless. She is trapped between life and death.

In Kan'ami's play *Komachi on the Sotoba (Sotoba Komachi)* Komachi finds escape in enlightenment. Her cosmic scheme becomes: Forsake-uni-dimensional life — lose ego — find enlightenment. Possessed and tormented by the ghost of her lover, she escapes despair by achieving a Zen satori. In true Zen fashion she celebrates her entrance into nirvana by performing a most unconventional act. Komachi sits on the sacred log, the sotoba, a procedure considered by the priests of the Shigon sect, who are rivals of the Zen Buddhists, sacrilegious. The priests taunt her for her deed, but Komachi turns their imprecations into Zen debating points celebrating her enlightenment:

| | |
|---|---|
| *Komachi:* | It [the sotoba] was on the ground already. What harm could it get by my resting on it? |
| *Priest:* | It was an act of discord. |
| *Komachi:* | Sometimes from discord salvation springs. |
| *Second Priest:* | That which is called Evil |
| *Komachi:* | Is Good. |
| *Priest:* | That which is called Illusion |
| *Komachi:* | Is Salvation |
| *Priest:* | For Salvation |
| *Komachi:* | Cannot be planted like a tree |
| *Priest:* | And the Heart's Mirror |
| *Komachi:* | Hangs in the void. |
| *Chorus:* | "Nothing is real. |
| *(speaking* | Between Buddha and Man |
| *for Komachi)* | Is no distinction but a seeming difference, planned |
| | For the welfare of the humble, the ill-instructed |
| | Whom he has vowed to save. |
| | Sin itself may be the ladder to salvation." |

> So she spoke eagerly: and the priests,
> "A saint, a saint is this decrepit, outcast soul."
> And bending their heads to the ground
> Three times did homage before her.[14]

The alternatives proposed by authors Kan'ami and Zeami of continuation of life without enlightenment, or death with enlightenment, admit to a further variation. If, as Buddhists teach, a continuum of life, the circle of samsara, goes on spinning forever and if one cannot escape into enlightenment, one may possess unwanted consciousness through an eternity of lifetimes. This grim knowledge is a subject both for contemplation and for exploration in modern Japanese literature.

[14]Kan'ami, *Sotoba Komachi*, trans. Arthur Waley in Arthur Waley, ed. *The Nō Plays of Japan*, pp. 154-55.

# CHAPTER XIV

## THE DESTRUCTION OF CONSCIOUSNESS: YUKIO MISHIMA

The possibility of infinite forced and undesired returns to earth by a spirit who has not achieved enlightenment is the subject of another play also entitled *Komachi on the Sobota* by the twentieth century Japanese writer Yukio Mishima (1925-1970). A fanatical superpatriot, Mishima, in despair that the politics of post-war Japan did not allow the nation to live up to his xenophobic goals, committed suicide by hari-kari.[1] As befits an ardent nationalist, Mishima was interested in the traditions of his country and experimented with writing traditional Nō dramas with twentieth century settings. Mishima's *Komachi on the Sobota* is not an adaptation of Kan'ami's play but a return to the original legend which centers upon Komachi's lover Captain Fukakusa and the hundredth night.

Mishima's *Komachi* opens with a view of a poverty-stricken old woman sitting on a park bench which replaces both the sacred log and the carriage shaft upon which the captain slept in earlier dramas involving the Komachi legend. The time is Japan of the 1950's. The woman's sparring partner is not a priest but a young poet who insults the bent figure on the park bench whom he comes upon counting her nightly haul of cigarette butts. The poet finds this wretched creature's presence in the flowering park incongruous. The park bench, he tells her, should be quickened by the presence of young lovers. When she, old and dying, sits on the park bench it becomes "just so many dreary slats of wood," but when ardent lovers are there, it could "become a memory . . . warm with sparks

---

[1] For details of Mishima's life and death see John Nathan, *Mishima* (Boston: Little, Brown, 1974).

thrown off by living people." Now it is as "old as a grave, like a beam put together out of slabs of tombstones."[2]

The poet cannot bear the presence of death which this aged crone epitomizes. The old woman tells him that his youth and inexperience blind him so that he cannot see that "those snotty-faced shop clerks with their whores over there are not truly alive but are making love on their graves." The flowers in the park have the smell of funeral flowers, "just like those inside a coffin. You and I are the only live ones."

The two fall into desultory small talk. The poet speaks of her vivacity in spite of her ninety-nine years (the one hundred nights of the legend have become one hundred years) and teasingly asks her reason for living. She answers that the fact of existing is reason itself.

The conversation has become serious:

| | |
|---|---|
| *Poet:* | Old lady, let me ask you something. Who are you? |
| *Old woman:* | Once I was a woman called Komachi. |
| *Poet:* | Who? |
| *Old woman:* | All of the men who said I was beautiful have died. Now I feel for sure that any man who says that I am beautiful will die. |

(p. 13)

The old woman tells him that years ago she was the epitome of grace and charm and adds that she is still a beauty even if she is an aged enchantress. But as a girl of nineteen — eighty years ago — she was irresistible, a femme fatale.

| | |
|---|---|
| *Poet:* | Tell me what happened eighty years ago, old woman. . . . |
| *Old woman:* | I was nineteen. Captain Fukakusa — he was at Staff Headquarters — was courting me. |
| *Poet:* | Shall I pretend to be Captain What's-his-name? |

---

[2]Yukio Mishima, *Sotoba Komachi* in *Kindai Nōgakushū*, trans. Donald Keene as *Five Modern Nō Plays* (New York: Knopf, 1957), pp. 8-9. Further references are in the text and give the page number of the Keene translation.

| | |
|---|---|
| *Old woman:* | Don't flatter yourself. He was a hundred times the man you are. . . . Yes, I told him I would grant what he desired if he visited me a hundred times. It was on the hundredth night. There was a ball at the Rokumei Hall. . . . |

(pp. 14-15)

A faint waltz melody becomes louder and Rokumei Hall, at first indistinct, is seen as background for a garden. The old woman is young again. Many at the ball comment on Komachi's beauty. The poet (as Captain Fukakusa) and Komachi dance. It is the hundredth night.

| | |
|---|---|
| *Poet* *(as in a dream):* | It's strange. . . . |
| *Old woman:* | What's strange? . . . . |
| *Poet:* | Somehow I. . . . |
| *Old woman:* | Please don't try to say it. I know what you want to say before you've said it. |
| *Poet* *(with ardor):* | You're — you're so — — |
| *Old woman:* | Beautiful — That's what you intended to say, isn't it? You mustn't. If you say it, you won't have long to live. That's fair warning. |

(pp. 20-21)

The setting is again the park in the 1950's. The poet is deliriously happy but he wonders in what kind of cycle he is caught. What if he should not gain the promise of the hundredth night? What if he must wait another hundred years? What if he should die? What is death? Is it the end of being? The old woman tells him that men do not live in order to die, and he counters that perhaps men die in order to live. He says that a transcendent moment is coming like the dream he once had of the sun at midnight and of a ship moving through the street. He knows that he must tell Komachi that she is beautiful even if he dies for it. She tries to stop his words by pointing to her ugly, wrinkled face, her mucus-filled eyes, the stench of her aged body. She takes his hand and presses it against her withered, dry breasts, but he tells her that the moment for which they have waited for ninety-nine years has come and blurts out:

> I'll tell you, Komachi. (*He takes her hand; she trembles.*) You are beautiful, the most beautiful woman in the world. Your beauty will not fade, not in ten thousand years.

(p. 31)

He knows that he and Komachi will meet again, but that the promise of the hundredth night will not be fulfilled until a century has passed when Komachi will again be near the end of her ninety-ninth year. He and Komachi will not have changed. Only the world will have altered. The old woman speaks to him:

> | *Old woman:* | You are an idiot. I can already see the mark of death between your eyebrows. |
> | *Poet:* | I don't want to die. |
> | *Old woman:* | I tried so hard to stop you. |
> | *Poet:* | My hands and feet have become cold. . . . I'll meet you again, I'm sure, in a hundred years, at the same place. |
> | *Old woman:* | A hundred years more to wait. (The poet's breathing ceases and he dies.) |

(p. 32)

The old woman is silent. As the curtain falls, she is seen collecting cigarette butts.

Mishima rewrites the basic equation again. For him it reads: man — enlightenment — beauty-as-destroyer-of-enlightenment. Beauty without enlightenment can pull one out of the life-and-death cycle temporarily but not long enough or strongly enough to prevent the necessity of re-entry. As long as beauty and death are in balance, the cycle continues. In terms of the here and now, as long as man yearns for beauty and not for satori, existence remains a life-and-death continuum. Life and death are wrapped up in and flavor each other.

For Mishima the question is: how does one destroy so strong a force as beauty and by means of that feat achieve nirvana? He presents his answer in his 1954 novel *The Temple of the Golden Pavilion.* His solution is worked out symbolically in the story of Mizoguchi, a young acolyte in a Zen Buddhist temple who burns the temple. Mishima had read a newspaper account of a young acolyte who had set fire to a famous temple in the ancient capital of Japan, the city of Kyoto. The motivations which caused Mizoguchi to turn pyromaniac form the warp and woof of the structure of the novel.

Mizoguchi was an unhappy child who grew into an even more wretched adult. He had been a shocked witness to his mother's lovemaking with her near relative. He does not grieve at the death of his father, a provincial priest who had apprenticed Mizoguchi to the temple.

Later he is unsuccessful with his superior whom he hates and with women. He is glad when a girl who had ignored him is tramped to death by a mob for defending a draft deserter. When a drunken American soldier in the occupation forces encourages him to stomp on the stomach of a prostitute whom the soldier has brought to see the temple, Mizoguchi does so. The girl, who is carrying the soldier's child, later dies in childbirth.

Mizoguchi is impotent with a young woman on whom he had once spied as she forced milk from her breast for her lover before he went to war and to his death. Mizoguchi develops a painful stutter. He ignores a nagging mother's urgings that he flatter his superior in order to take his place when the superior retires. Instead Mizoguchi lets his superior know that Mizoguchi has seen him with a geisha girl in the red light district.

With no hope of advancement, Mizoguchi sees the temple as both his prison and the summation of the evil within him. Yet the edifice has a fascination for him because of its transcendent beauty. The structure dominates his mind until it becomes an obsession. He comes to see it as the symbol of the failures of his past and as the essence of his wounding separateness from life. He concludes that as long as the temple endures, he cannot be fully alive and resolves to destroy it and the beauty it represents. With the decision he feels himself potent, goes to a prostitute, and loses his virginity. He purchases arsenic and a knife in case he is discovered and must commit suicide.

Gazing at the Golden Temple, and bidding it a last farewell, he is almost overcome by its transcendent beauty. As first person narrator, Mizoguchi explains his reaction:

. . . Yet I did not know whether beauty was, on the one hand, identical with the Golden Temple itself, or on the other consubstantial with the night of nothingness that surrounded the temple. Perhaps beauty was both these things . . . . At this thought, I felt that the mystery of the temple, which had tormented me so much in the past, was half way toward being solved. If one examined the beauty of the individual details . . . . the beauty was never completed in any single detail . . .: for each detail adumbrated the beauty of the succeeding detail. The beauty of the individual detail itself was always filled with uneasiness. It dreamed of perfection, but it knew no completion and was invariably lured on to the next beauty, the unknown beauty. The adumbration of beauty contained in one detail was linked with the subsequent adumbration of beauty, and so it was that the various adumbrations of beauty *which did not exist* had become the underlying motif of the Golden Temple. Such adumbrations were the sign of nothingness. Nothingness was the very structure of this beauty . . . . There arose automatically an adumbration of nothingness, and this delicate building, wrought from the most slender timber, was trembling in anticipation of nothingness, like a jeweled necklace trembling in the wind.

Yet never did there come a time when the beauty of the Golden Temple ceased! Its beauty was always echoing somewhere . . . . I invariably heard the sound of the Golden Temple's beauty wherever I might be, and I had grown accustomed to it . . . . But what if the sound should stop?[3]

Mizoguchi hesitates, falters, and almost denies his resolution to destroy the temple. As his mind struggled to grasp the essence of the beauty of the temple, he was also attempting to bring to his conscious mind words he had learned as an acolyte, for these words were trying to approach him to put him "on his mettle":

"Face the back, face the outside, and if you meet, kill instantly."
Yes, first sentence went like that. The famous passage of that chapter of the *Rinsairokū*. Then the remaining words emerged

---

[3]Yukio Mishima, *Kinkakuji* (1954), trans. Ivan Morris as *The Temple of the Golden Pavilion* (New York: Knopf, 1959), pp. 254-55. Further references are in the text and give the page number of the Morris translation.

fluently: "When ye meet the Buddha, kill the Buddha! When ye meet your ancestor, kill your ancestor! When ye meet a disciple of Buddha, kill the disciple of Buddha! When ye meet your mother and father, kill your mother and father! When ye meet your kin, kill your kin! Only thus will ye obtain deliverance. Only thus will ye escape trammels of material things and become free!"

These words propelled me out of the impotence into which I had fallen. All of a sudden my whole body was infused with strength. One part of my mind kept telling me that it was futile to perform the deed, but my newfound strength had no fear of futility. I must do the deed precisely because it was so futile.

(p. 258)

Mizoguchi sets fire to the temple. He escapes and hides:

I looked into my pocket and extracted the bottle of arsenic, wrapped in my handkerchief, and the knife, and threw them down the ravine. But then I noticed the pack of cigarettes in my other pocket. I took one out and started smoking it. I felt like a man who settles down for a smoke after finishing a job of work. I wanted to live.

(p. 262)

These are the last words of the novel. A madman has destroyed a great treasure of world art. Sane people everywhere would join every true Buddhist in condemning the deed. Muzoguchi had broken with the ethics of right living embodied in the eightfold path. The passage in the *Rinsairokū* is not a call to action. It is a command to wrest the mind free from itself by means of shocking thought in order to obtain satori. One cannot be enlightened until he escapes such common logic as "I love my parents and therefore I cannot kill them." Only after one is free from a system in which killing is possible, only after one's mind is so changed that he could not kill anyone, and certainly not the Buddha who is enlightenment, can the mind be so free of logic that it can be truly enlightened.

What is of interest here is not Mizoguchi's misinterpretation of Buddhist scripture, his perversion of Buddhist ethics, or his crime. Rather it is the solution that Mishima offers. In order for the sequence man-life-beauty to become man-life-enlightenment, beauty must be destroyed. If all the beauty in the world can be imagined in one object which is destroyed, a hypothetical case which Mizoguchi in his own mind converts to reality, beauty will be no more, and one can no longer love it. By destroying the love of beauty in one's own mind, one forces the mind into enlightenment.

The tale ends here as Buddhist-inspired tales must. If one's life ends in satori, the condition is beyond good and evil, beyond cause and effect. It is not consciousness as humans know it. It is not absence of consciousness, either. It is not life as humans know it. It is not death, either. It is something else. Having become something else, it ceases to be describable in human terms. The metaconscious experience becomes total and at the same moment disappears. The experience does not in the human mind function completely. It has for a few Buddhist saints by their own testimony been in part and at times realized.

It has been stated here that the new views of twentieth century physics have allowed Western minds to admit a new hospitality toward interpretations of consciousness found in certain non-Western cultures. It is possible to seek to translate a Buddhist theory of consciousness into Western terms. A Buddhist history of consciousness would end where a Western one begins and begin where a Western history ends. Historian of science Sir William Cecil Dampier has noted that to the Buddhist the high point in the development of life as sketched by Western scientists would not be the multiplicity of forms, including human beings, which flourish throughout the earth in our day, but rather that first primeval cell of life that emerged from the tropical sea in the beginning.[4] To the Buddhist the great diversity of life which came after that first primeval cell has been downhill all the way.

Again, Western theories of consciousness usually include an account of the development of the brain as the seat of consciousness. In a Buddhist theory consciousness can begin only when the brain ceases functioning in a normal way and when the essence of being escapes from the physical body. In the Newtonian world of a clockwork universe, Buddhist ideas had no place in the West. But Einstein and the quantum physicists

---

[4]William Cecil Dampier, *A History of Science*, 4th ed. (1929; Cambridge: Cambridge Univ. Press, 1949), pp. 319-20.

shattered the Newtonian world. Now it is possible in the West to entertain the possibility that consciousness may in fact somehow be, at least in part, exogenous to the human body. As Julian Jaynes puts it:

> Actually you could, as you remain where you are, just as well locate your consciousness around the corner in the next room against the wall near the floor, and do your thinking there as well as in your head. Not really just as well. For there are very good reasons why it is better to imagine your mind-space inside of you, reasons to do with volition and internal sensations, with the relationship of your body and your 'I' . . . .[5]

With a Newtonian world picture such a statement would be absurd. But in the post-Einsteinian world, it begins to have possibilities which are explored as these theories are reflected in a modern myth of consciousness based on late twentieth-century scientific hypotheses.

---

[5] Jaynes, *The Origin of Consciousness in the Breakdown of the Bicameral Mind*, p. 46.

# CHAPTER XV

## NATURE TRANSFORMED:
## THE BLACK HOLE OF THE MIND

In the 1960's astronomers discovered high energy sources of radio waves located, from the standpoint of the size of the cosmos, relatively near the earth in our galaxy. These sources, which are called pulsars, are believed to come from huge stars, some of which are so large that they have run out of fuel and can no longer spew matter and energy into the universe. Instead, matter and energy implode with tremendous force as the huge star shrinks inward, crashing in on itself. According to Einstein's general theory of relativity, space and time can become warped by the presence of matter in much the same way that wrinkles in a bed sheet can distort a smooth well-made bed. According to a theory which is becoming more and more plausible to astronomers, so violent are the explosions of these giant stars that the very laws of gravity and matter become warped. Matter, space, and time collapse. The result is what is called a *black hole* in space.

Black holes have never been discovered, but mathematicians and astronomers working on the mathematics of black holes have postulated that they exist. In the 1960's Roy P. Kerr formulated for a black hole equations that would exhibit both mass and angular momentum and a measure of rotation.[1]

In 1960 Roger Penrose invented a technique called conformal mapping by means of which not only space and time within a black hole but also the relationship of the black hole to other

---

[1]For a non-technical discussion of Kerr's work, and for the tracing of a route astronauts might follow through a black hole, see William J. Kaufmann, III, *The Cosmic Frontiers of General Relativity* (Boston: Little, Brown, 1977), pp. 213-19.

parts of the universe could be mapped.[2] If anything fell into a black hole, it would at first be pulled in at terrific speed. In Einstein's special theory of relativity, time is a function of the speed of light. No absolute time frame exists, but each observer records an event as it comes to him by means of vision (light waves) or by means of some other waves (radio waves, a type of radiation which travels as fast as light, but no faster). In a black hole the force of gravity would be so great that it would not allow light to escape. To an observer outside the black hole watching a body plunging into it, the object would appear to stop and no light would escape. This point is called the *event horizon*. Finally, at the center of the black hole, time and space would have an infinite curvature, and the gravitational field would become infinite. That point is called the *singularity*.

At the singularity, it would seem that anything smashed by infinite gravity would disintegrate. However, if one applies Penrose's diagrams to Kerr's description of a black hole, it seems possible that a traveler through a black hole might avoid the singularity and emerge into another universe, perhaps in our universe in the future, or a completely different one, governed, for instance, by anti-gravity. According to this theory, an infinite number of such universes may be linked together.[3] If the theory of time travel through a black hole should be correct, perhaps there are also huge outpourings of matter from a past universe into our universe of the here and now. Such a possible outpouring is termed a *white hole*.[4]

In the 1970's certain scientists have objected to the idea of the possibility of travel through time or through great distances of space by way of a black hole. D. M. Eardley of the California Institute of Technology believes that blue light energy around a white hole would pull the white hole back into the black hole again. Stephen W. Hawking of Cambridge University has said that the potential matter-producing proclivities of warped space-time around the singularity would quickly, according to Einstein's theory of the equivalence of energy and matter, change the energy into matter which would come

---

[2] Ibid., p. 142.
[3] Ibid., pp. 186-87.
[4] Ibid., pp. 240-41.

spewing out around the singularity. Such matter would consist of particles and anti-particles (which display opposite physical features to the particles with which they are paired). The particles and anti-particles would choke off the areas of alternate universes mapped by the Penrose diagram, and blue light would prevent white holes from being formed. Therefore travel through a black hole to other times and places would, if Eardley and Hawking are correct, be impossible.[5]

If it turns out that black holes do not provide rapid highways across intergalactic distances, the possibility of the intergalactic travel of ideas through an exchange of information with other galaxies cannot be ruled out. Scientists already possess the radio telescope, an instrument which is capable of sending signals which can cross intergalactic distances at the speed of light.

Black holes and intergalactic communication compose a set of as yet undiscovered facts. As has been noted earlier, all science contains a bit of mythology in that every time a scientist proposes a new hypothesis, he has on his hands what might be called a myth, a hypothesis which has not yet been tested against the facts.[6] The scientist works as quickly as possible to change his theory from hypothesis to fact. The mythmaker, whose myth finds its validity within a belief system and not in facts, can afford to ignore the facts if he so chooses. In modern times, science and mythology have remained separate disciplines.

Today when astrophysicists and other scientists speculate about black holes and about intergalactic research, they are at the cutting edge of the frontiers of science. Their speculations concern a body of conjectures which have the rigor of scientific proof, yet such esoteric sciences as black hole research are closer today to mythology than science has been since the Renaissance. Scientists writing about black holes have no more proof than a myth-intoxicated writer who centers a mythic plot around black holes and intergalactic adventures. In that sense,

---

[5] Ibid., pp. 243-47.

[6] For a discussion of scientific hypothesis as a form of myth, see Mary Hesse, *The Structure of Scientific Inference* (Berkeley: Univeristy of California Press, 1974), p. 32.

science and mythology may be said to be — however temporarily — reunited.

One of the subjects of great popular interest in the twentieth century is the possibility of life on other planets. The scientist or mythmaker , or,  as he might be called, the scientific mythmaker looks at black holes or at other avenues of communication, such as radiotelescopy, to get in touch with the stars and ponders the possibility of communication with intelligent life on other planets. If conscious life is discovered on other planets, the case might be made for a new leaf in the book of the history of consciousness, the case for exosomatic consciousness — forms of consciousness other than those found inside the human brain.

In the past, many thinkers, among them the philosophers Leibnitz and Kant, speculated concerning the possibility of existence on other planets, but there never has been, in the past or today, any evidence, direct or indirect, of life in any other place in the universe. Statistical studies show that our galaxy, if one includes an accompanying star cluster called the Magellanic Clouds, is about two hundred thousand light years across. Taking our sun as an average star, and assuming that about ninety percent of the mass of our galaxy is located near the galactic center, astronomers assume that from one hundred to one hundred fifty billion stars are in our galaxy alone. In 1923 the American astronomer Edwin Powell Hubble, using a newly installed, powerful telescope at the Mt. Wilson observatory in California, was able to show that a huge cloud far beyond our galaxy called the Andromeda Nebula, which had earlier been thought to consist of dust, is also composed of stars.[7] It is now estimated that in the visible universe alone there are billions and perhaps hundreds of billions of galaxies.

Given Oparin's thesis discussed earlier that life evolved on earth from inanimate matter, it seemed inevitable that someone would play the game of statistics and create a science of *exobiology*, the study of possibilities of life on other planets. In the late 1970's, the beginnings of the science called

---

[7]For an account of Hubble's discoveries see Asimov, *The Universe: From Flat Earth to Quasar*, p. 105.

*exopsychology,* the study of the possibility of conscious life else-where in the universe, has come into being.

A major book published on the subject of exobiology appeared in 1962. Written by the Soviet scientist Iosef Shklovskii, it was titled *Life, Mind and the Universe.* It was translated by Paula Fern and revised for publication in America by Carl Sagan under the title *Intelligent Life in the Universe.* In 1973 Sagan, working alone, published a popularization of exobiology called *The Cosmic Connection.*

The Shklovskii-Sagan hypothesis rests on the mathematics of the gigantic size of the universe and the fact that the star which is nearest our sun appears to have a planet circling it. In outline, the theory is as follows: given the limitless stars in the universe, many are so large that they consume everything around them. But some are not so large that they burn everything up, and not too small to give out sufficient energy to support life. Out of the latter category, the probabilities are that many hundreds of billions have one or more planets, some of which will contain atmosphere close enough to earth to support hydrogen and carbon, or perhaps some other element, such as silicon, which, following Oparin's theory, will allow life to evolve on these planets. Among the planets which can support life, the statistical probabilities are that on some of them some form of intelligent life exists. Some planets may have creatures intelligent enough to be of interest to us. Perhaps some have societies or races of beings who are superior to humans in intelligence and in behavior.

If there are planets with intelligent societies, why have we never had messages from any of them? One answer is that they are very far away. Previously in human history, humans did not have radio transmission, the one form of communication which can span interplanetary distances. (Marconi invented the wireless in 1906.) If there is intelligent life on other planets, it may be radically different from ours. Shklovskii made two assumptions about at least some of the intelligent societies which might exist. The first is that if the same electromagnetic laws of communication work throughout the universe, intelligent creatures will eventually discover these laws and will be able to communicate with each other. The second assumption is that on some of these planets social creatures live and on some planets not every inhabitant will be a hermit. Societies with civilizations which build up stores of information will be formed on these planets.

Shklovskii and Sagan have assumed that beings on some other planets will be intelligent and that they will be willing and able to communicate with us. But so great are the distances between the planets which orbit around different stars that the information from a radio message from another planet might take billions of years to reach us. If and when we do receive messages, they may have taken so long to travel that the civilization which sent them may already have perished. If those civilizations no longer exist, the loss can be tolerated. Sagan cites Philip Morrison of MIT who notes that we still communicate with the ancient Greeks even if it is only a one-way communication from their past to our present.[8]

If, on the other hand, we on earth are ever able to build telescopes powerful enough to reach other living creatures, and if we have the serendipity to discover intelligent life on other planets, we may find beings much simpler than we, so that they would by our standards be uninteresting as communication partners. Nonetheless, they would be fascinating as beings for study. (Human entomologists sometimes spend lifetimes studying ants.) It is probable that the first civilizations that we reach will also have message-sending devices, that is, that these creatures will have invented radio telescopes.

The two criteria, Sagan reasons, for a civilization to serve as our communication partner are that the civilization would have enough power and technology to reach us, and enough knowledge to interest us. (Conceivably our civilization might seem like a colony of ants to an advanced civilization but perhaps aliens would consider us intelligent ants.) In order to measure the two criteria and to rate potential communication partners, Sagan adopts a scale for power rating based on the work of the Soviet astrophysicist N. S. Kardashev.[9] In

---

[8]Cited in Carl Sagan, *The Cosmic Connection* (1973: paperback ed. rpt. New York: Dell, 1975), p. 218.

[9]For a discussion of the Kardashev-Sagan method of correlating power output and information storage capacities, see Sagan, *The Cosmic Connection*, pp. 233-39.

order to reach us, the alien civilization, according to Kardashev, must have enough power to be entered on a scale which ranges from 1 to 4. Any number less than 1 on the scale means that the other civilization does not have a powerful enough energy system to reach us. The planet earth today is at number 0.7 on the scale. Those civilizations which would be classified 4 could communicate at will anywhere in the entire universe.

To measure the amount of information a civilization would need in order to be an interesting communication partner, Sagan adopts from computer and information science the concept of a *bit* of information. A bit answers each of a series of a twenty-question formula with a *yes* or a *no*, as in the example "Is he living?" Each question answered *yes* or *no* is a *bit* of information. If a civilization contained enough information to interest us, it would enter Sagan's scale which ranges from $A$ to $Z$. For instance, the early civilization of ancient Greece in this classification was rated $C$. The amount of information is not a measure of how stimulating the society is.(Ancient Greece was one of the most fascinating of all human cultures.) If one takes into account the total amount of information on the planet earth, the classification is $H$. Through a combination of information with the measure of broadcasting power, the planet is at $0.7H$. The maximum which the system could possess is $4Z$ which would represent a super-civilization.

Many advanced peoples might exist so far from us that unless a special kind of communication link, as, for instance, a passage through a black hole, could be established, we would never be able to know that they are in the universe. Others, however, might be close enough so that some day we could get in touch with them. Such conjectures lay the groundwork for modern myths.

# CHAPTER XVI

## CONSCIOUSNESS IN THE STARS

It is not surprising that with such sciences as exobiology and exopsychology already crossing the border into mythology, myths which deal seriously with questions of alien civilizations have appeared. One of the more interesting mythic themes concerns communication with aliens which, unknown to us, may either already have occurred or is about to happen.

There are good myths and bad myths, weak myths and strong ones. One genre of weak mythology is that of the ilk offered by Erich von Däniken who proposes that in earlier times our civilization was visited by aliens, and that various monuments, such as the Mayan ruins and the Pyramids, were constructed under their supervision. Far more plausible theories concerning the building of these great architectural monuments do not depend upon extraterrestial intervention.

A trend of thought which has produced a more serious and a better mythology offers the thesis that perhaps the aliens have been waiting for humans to develop a civilization advanced enough so that they would consider us worthwhile communication partners. It is sometimes assumed that only in the last quarter of the twentieth century is our civilization on earth approaching the breakthrough point.

Such is the theme of *2001: A Space Odyssey*, a motion picture directed by Stanley Kubrick whose collaborator Arthur C. Clarke wrote a novel based on the film. [Unless otherwise indicated, the novel, not the film, is discussed below.[1]] The

[1]See Arthur C. Clarke, *2001: A Space Odyssey* (New York: New American Library, 1968), based on a screenplay by Arthur C. Clarke and Stanley Kubrick for the 1968 motion picture *2001: A Space Odyssey* directed by Stanley Kubrick.

central thrust of the book is that at a critical juncture in man's development while he still exhibited proto-man-ape characteristics, a superior race somewhere far out in the universe set a machine in our world in the form of a metal obelisk which temporarily took over the minds of a group of earthlings and gave them a mental leap forward, allowing them and their progeny to evolve successfully into men. Burying a similar disk on the moon, the aliens assumed that by the time men reached the moon, they would be prepared to leap forward into evolution again.

From prehistoric scenes of early mindless man, trying to manipulate stone tools, dragging a leopard to a cave for food, and attempting to use a bone as a primitive weapon, time shifts to the year 2001 and a world plagued with nuclear proliferation and vast overpopulation. On the moon a small group of Americans, part of a Soviet-American exploring team, discover the obelisk buried by the aliens.

Remembering American reaction to Orson Welles' broadcast in the 1930's concerning the landing of aliens, and the various polls which indicate that men have innate hostility toward alien intelligence, and considering the possibilities of military danger from aliens, the team keeps the discovery secret.

A piercing screech of high frequency emanating from the obelisk is thought to be related to a mysterious wave whose source is on a moon of Saturn. On earth a special space ship, commanded by David Bowman and carrying six astronauts, four of whom are in suspended animation, is launched. Plot complications, when the thinking, talking computer Hal goes berserk and kills all the astronauts except Bowman who prevents Hal from killing him by pulling Hal's plug, provide intrigue. Although an important issue — man's ability to control his own technology — is addressed, it is not central to a discussion of human consciousness but toys with the possibility of man-made consciousness going awry.

Bowman approaches the moon of Saturn and sees another obelisk filled with stars floating ahead of him. This obelisk is the gateway to a black hole which Bowman enters. Escaping the singularity in the black hole, he discovers that aliens use the black hole as a cosmic switching station. He emerges from the black hole in another time and space.

Authors Kubrick and Clarke had been at a loss concerning how the new universe and the aliens would look to human eyes. Various ideas were considered and rejected: a meeting with a spinning ballet dancer; an involved tour of alien cities; a man-like form which would offer to shake hands with Bowman.[2] At one point Carl Sagan was called in. Sagan explained that, given the many paths that evolution might take, it is impossible to picture the appearance or the conduct of aliens with any accuracy.[3] Finally it was decided that the aliens would prepare a reception room for Bowman similar to a drawing room on earth.

In the movie the aliens do not appear. Instead Bowman's ship lands on a giant building with French Restoration interior decor. Books are merely bookcovers, and the non-toxic nourishing food all has the same flavor. The TV programs are a few years old. The aliens are trying to help Bowman overcome cultural shock. They have great things in store for him.

Bowman quickly grows older and older but instead of dying, he becomes a small wrinkled baby — a star child who has been programmed by the obelisk to return to earth to give humans another great leap in intelligence. As the babe begins his journey to earth in an artificial womb, his eyes are open. He is going back home as a transformed human being to spread the word. He is not sure what the word will be but, in the last words of the novel: "He would think of something."[4]

Who are the aliens? Clarke says that he based his concept of them on the more imaginative speculations of earth biologists. An alien race, remote and intelligent, had gambled that humans and other equivalent forms of life on many planets have the potential to become godlike and that they might survive and reach the stage which would enable them to become star

---

[2]For a discussion of the problems of making the picture, including the ways which were taken under consideration to portray the aliens, and some of the plot sequences later deleted from the script, see Arthur C. Clarke, *The Lost Worlds of "2001"* (New York: New American Library, 1972).

[3]See Sagan, *The Cosmic Connection*, pp. 181-82.

[4]Clarke, *2001: A Space Odyssey*, p. 221.

children. These beings assumed that humans had such a possibility when the first obelisk was sent to earth in the Pleistocene era. At that time the aliens often made errors concerning their estimates of potentially intelligent species on various planets, but in the centuries since the Pleistocene era, the aliens, too, have made progress. By the year 2001 they no longer make mistakes. Clarke speculates concerning the progress of alien evolution. Their first major step beyond the already awesome achievement of intergalactic space travel is the capacity to attach brains to artificial bodies in far more sophisticated versions of the crude transplants and artificial limbs offered by earth surgeons of our era. With bodies serving as space ships, the aliens can roam the stars. As humans become star children, they will have the capability to evolve in ways similar to the accomplishments of the aliens. Clarke conjectures concerning the ultimate course of human evolution:

> And eventually the brain might go. As the seat of consciousness, it was not essential: the development of electronic intelligence had proved that. The conflict between mind and machine might be resolved at last in the eternal truths of complete symbiosis. . . .
>
> But was even this the end? A few mystically inclined biologists went still further. They speculated, taking their cues from the beliefs of many religions, that mind would eventually free itself from matter. The robot body, like the flesh-and-blood one, would be no more than a stepping stone to something which, long ago, men had called "spirit."
>
> And if there was anything beyond *that*, its name could only be God.[5]

These words approach the mythic heart of *2001*. If man met alien intelligence, the age-old man-nature-God trilogy would have to be rewritten again as human being — extraterrestrial being or beings — nature — God. Kubrick and Clarke speculate that one of the alternatives for the equation may be: human beings — extraterrestial nature — Divinity. Extraterrestial nature would play the role in the new science that God has historically played in religion. The substitution does not mean that alien beings would replace God. They would instead be as God as our minds would come to conceive of God. In an interview with Eric Norden, Kubrick said:

> I will say that the God concept is at the heart of *2001* — but not any traditional, anthropomorphic image of God. I don't believe in any of the earth's monotheistic religions, but I do believe that one can construct an intriguing *scientific* definition of God, once you accept the fact that there are approximately one hundred billion stars in our galaxy alone, that each star is a life-giving sun, and that there are approximately one hundred billion galaxies in just the *visible* universe. Given a planet in a stable orbit, not too hot and not too cold, and given a few billion years of chance chemical reactions created by the interactions of the sun's energy on the planet's chemicals, it's fairly certain that life in one form or another will eventually emerge.[6]

In the views of many scientists, it is logical to assume that on countless billions of planets biological life has already developed, and that the chances are high that there are intelligent beings on many of these planets. In Kubrick's words:

> It's reasonable to assume that there must be, in fact, countless *billions* of such planets where biological life has arisen, and the odds of some proportion of such life developing intelligence are high. Now, the sun is by no means an old star, and its planets are mere children in cosmic age, so it seems likely that there are billions of planets in the universe, not only where intelligent life is on a lower scale than man, but other billions where it is approximately equal and others still where it is hundreds of thousands of millions of years in advance of us.[7]

The great technological advances that man has made in the last few millenia, which is a period of less than a micro-second in the chronology of the universe, furnish some intimation of the possible evolutionary development that older life forms may have reached:

> They may have progressed from biological species, which are fragile shells for the mind at best, into immortal machine entities — and then, over innumerable eons, they could emerge from the chrysalis of matter transformed into beings of pure

[6]Eric Norden, "*Playboy*, Interview: Stanley Kubrick," *Playboy*, 15, No. 9 (Sept., 1968), 94.
[7]Ibid.

energy and spirit. Their potentialities would be limitless and
their intelligence ungraspable by humans.[8]

Norden asked, interviewing Kubrick, "Even assuming the
cosmic evolutionary path you suggest, what has this to do with
the nature of God?", and the answer came that it has everything to do with the nature of God because these creatures
would possess two of the attributes man has given to the deity
— omniscience and omnipotence. They could perhaps have
telepathic communication with events throughout the universe. They might be able to tap every intelligent mind with as
little effort as humans turn on television. They might have
power to travel faster than the speed of light so that they could
have representatives in every far corner of the universe. They
might develop mastery over matter and energy. Kubrick offers
an even more transcendent achievement:

> They might develop into an integrated collective immortal con-
> sciousness. They would be incomprehensible to us except as
> gods: and if the tendrils of their consciousness ever brushed
> men's minds, it is only the hand of God we could grasp as an
> explanation.[9]

Clarke proposes that there is room for human immortality in
this system. Our lives are not yet ready for immortality, but the
memory system which is the necessary basis of neural functioning exists, not only to give man a past but to help him make
sense of the present, and to provide tertiary hypothetical
reasoning out of which he can construct the future. In Clarke's
system, memory is more. As Bowman prepares to become a
star child, he notices that a most curious process is occurring.
Instead of the customary recognition of the forward passing of
time, it seemed to Bowman that time was running backward.
He comprehended what Clarke has called a "subtler truth,"
that as his life unreeled like an ever-accelerating tape recorder,
Bowman's memory was being drained of knowledge and experience:

> But nothing was being lost: all that he had ever been, at every
> moment of his life, was being transferred to safer keeping. Even

---

[8]Ibid.
[9]Ibid.

as one Dave Bowman ceased to exist, another became immortal.[10]

Is it possible that human memory, an integral consciousness, is also functioning as a plan to store life, and that our memories are a first step toward our immortality? Such speculations at this point can only be mythic. Several cautions occur. If there is no telepathy possible between mortals and aliens, or if there are alien intelligences but no black holes through which they can move safely at a speed faster than light, such power of intercommunication throughout the cosmos and such capacity for memory storage for immortality would prove impossible. Writing of such limitations, Sagan reflects:

> In a way, St. Augustine and many other thoughtful theologians have come to rather the same conclusions — God must not live from moment to moment, but during all times simultaneously. That is, in a way, the same thing as saying that special relativity did not apply to Him. But supercivilization gods, perhaps the only ones that this kind of scientific speculation admits, are limited. There may be such gods of galaxies, but not of the universe as a whole.[11]

To these limitations others can be added. Not only is it possible that we may never make contact with alien civilizations: it is also possible, though not probable, that earth is the only place in the universe where life exists. There may be no time travel or black holes, either. If hypotheses remain forever unrealized, exopsychology will forever remain the stuff of mythology.

Even if we must assume that exopsychology will always be without the realm of science, the concept contributes to our understanding of the nature of consciousness. The essence of the term exopsychology is in the prefix *exo – from without*. If it is assumed that the mind will never through evolution free itself from the brain, one may still wonder whether nature has ever looked upon consciousness as being limited only to the brain, in the first place.

Edwin Land, the inventor of the Polaroid camera, recently

---

[10]Clarke, *2001: A Space Odyssey*, p. 216.
[11]Sagan, *The Cosmic Connection*, p. 243.

stated that the science of optics is calling for a new theory of consciousness. Land discussed his childhood memories of the stereoscope at home in which a flat picture when placed in a viewer would suddenly take on three dimensions. Since childhood, Land related, he had pondered the locale of that third dimension and had recently concluded that it is an error to consider the third dimension only a trick of the mind. Rather it took billions of years of a special kind of evolution to create not only the eyes, which act as stereoscopic receptors, but a material world which would be made in such a way that three-dimensional viewing of it could be possible![12]

Can it be that when we discuss alien intelligence, we are speaking of something far closer to home, mother nature herself? The astronomer J. Allen Hynek, scientific advisor to the director of another motion picture on the subject of aliens, *Close Encounters of the Third Kind*, has speculated that when flying saucer fanatics say that they have seen aliens, one explanation is that what they really see may not come from outer space at all but from a kind of neo-Jungian inner space, a new and as yet undetermined and unexplored dimension of their own minds.[13]

Perhaps the ancient tension between man and nature and deity, a trichotomy which has been the subject of explorers of consciousness for so long, is about to wear out its usefulness. The realization that we are truly a part of nature and that we are also in some ways divine allows us to see that the explanation of consciousness may lie in the acceptance of the truism that when we shall have learned more about the human mind, we will know a great deal more about the universe.[14]

---

[12] See Edwin Land, "Our 'Polar Partnership' With the World Around Us," *Harvard Magazine*, 80, No. 3 (Jan.-Feb., 1978), 25.
[13] See J. Allen Hynek, *The UFO Experience* (Chicago: Regnery, 972), p. 4.
[14] Kaufmann, *Relativity and Cosmology*, p. 126.

# CHAPTER XVII

## CONSCIOUSNESS: A PROSPECTIVE VIEW

A short summary of this study indicates that a common bond between its parts — science and literary mythology — exists. It has been seen that consciousness involves both the higher brain processes and self-awareness. The structural anthropology of Claude Lévi-Strauss allows mind to be viewed as an object in the universe. Sir Karl Popper holds that the universe, although chance plays a great part in its workings, is guided by statistical probabilities, and that consciousness arose when matter began to solve problems. One form of man's efforts at problem-solving is myth.

In adopting a biological and mythological definition of consciousness from critical realism, it is not being argued here that the long history of philosophy in the West had nothing to do with producing that definition, or that critical realism did not come to its conclusions in part by reinforcing or by rejecting certain aspects of previous philosophical thought. Sir Karl Popper's position of critical realism would not have been possible in its present form without Plato, Aristotle, Kant, and other philosophers who came before this modern philosopher who, as a part of Western philosophical tradition, now augments, now opposes, now revises aspects of that heritage. Yet a definition of consciousness derived from Popper's critical realism and from the structuralism of Claude Lévi-Strauss that consciousness is in part an ability of human beings, physical creatures, to produce problem-solving and self-defining myths comes closer than any other theses yet formulated toward making progress in solving the riddles of the mind/body problem.

The universe, it is now believed, began some twenty to fifteen billion years ago. Some cosmologists hold that plan may have existed from the first split second after the universe began as a result of a greater-than-chance confluence of events which kept all the hydrogen in the universe from becoming helium, a conversion which would have prevented the existence of the universe.

Sir Fred Hoyle, reviving the ideas of Ernst Mach, indicates that plan is imposed locally on earth by the rest of the matter in the universe. Most scientists today would agree that, whether or not plan existed at the beginning of the universe, life itself is a plan, a program imposed upon matter.

On earth a genetic programming material DNA evolved from inanimate matter. Through the agency of DNA, life insures both its own continuation and the individuality of each organism. After the formation of DNA and life, one-celled and then multi-celled plants and animals arose.

The development of the nervous system in animals heralded the beginnings of consciousness. Mammals evolved sophisticated brains capable of processing many channels of information through receptors in several senses. But even the brightest primates lacked the capability of self-realization. That all-important distinction was reserved for man.

*Homo habilis*, an ancestor of modern man, had simple tools and the beginnings of a capacity for language and for a subjective mind.

*Homo erectus*, who came later, developed the ability to think in sentences. He acquired a primitive technology and added tertiary or hypothetical imagination to augment the primary world of the senses and the secondary private world. He formulated a language with syntax which was able to mirror changes in the world that a transformation such as fire had caused.

With the appearance of *Homo sapiens* man became conscious in the sense that he possessed both the higher brain functions and self-awareness, at least in rudimentary form. He knew that he was mortal. He began to bury his dead. He practiced religion.

Modern man, *Homo sapiens sapiens*, who ruled the earth during the last fifty thousand years, has created art, mathematics, advanced technology, urban civilization, and writing. He has achieved awareness of self as an individual. Because of his capacity to invent myths which have helped him explain the mysteries both in himself and in his universe, he is able to see himself as a mythic creature. He possesses quarternary imagination which has allowed him not only to be conscious but to study his consciousnesss. His language has become a symbolic system.

With the advent of modern man, science alone cannot completely describe the thought processess because science does not have a vocabulary to deal with myth. Mythical aspects of life can best be approached through the study of man as mythmaker. Especially useful are those literary myths which are specifically concerned with human consciousness.

The mythic imagination creates what sociologist Robert Bellah has called symbolic reality which treats the universe and man as systems of symbols. J.R.R. Tolkien has argued that artistic myths are a function of sub-creation, the ability of the human to create a counter-world which has ontological validity, which alternates with the reality of daily life, and which is a contribution to the "gross national product" of the universe.

Modern Western man did not come by his mythic understanding easily and quickly. Homer thought that the mind acted in ways analogous to the functioning of a physical organ. The early Greek lyric poets introduced a subjective *you* into the cosmos. The pre-Socratic philosophers reduced the universe to an *it*.

The Greek playwrights in the Golden Age explored in myth the price man pays for consciousness. In *Prometheus Bound*, Aeschylus lauded self-awareness and creativity as forms of human divinity while he regretted man's estrangement from nature and his awareness of death. Sophocles saw man's consciousness as a form of alienation. Humans themselves became potential sources of pollution. Fate and determinism undermined man's freedom.

Plato's philosophical myths served to counterbalance the pessimism of the Greek tragedians. Plato viewed mind as a physical expression of an eternal soul. He unwittingly midwifed the birth of psychology, a discipline continued by Aristotle. Western man's study of consciousness would ultimately become not only mythic, but philosophical and scientific.

In the West in the Middle Ages before modern science and philosophy were born, mythic subjects continued to serve as vehicles for the exploration of consciousness. The theories found in Greek myths were combined with those of the Hebrews and the Christians. The Judeo-Christian tradition saw man's consciousness as a natural process but also as a prize stolen from God. Later Jewish thought developed eschatological hopes for first the nation and then for the individual. Jesus taught that the Christian could in essence experience a double consciousness. While living in a world of sin, the Christian could in his quaternary imagination participate in the coming kingdom of heaven.

In the Middle Ages the concept of consciousness was blended with that of conscience. Death and sin were the wages of those who went against the dictates of a Christian cosmos. Consciousness became an ethical dimension and supplied the feeble eyes by which mere man could view the majesty and the awe of God.

In early modern times Copernican and Newtonian laws reduced physics and astronomy to mechanism, but literary mythology reflected an idealistic philosophy which countered the Newtonian world view by seeing mind no longer as a natural, but as a supernatural entity.

In the philosophy of some of his characters Shakespeare celebrated mind as a capacity which gave man divine power while at the same time he acknowledged the supernatural abilities of mind in its preoccupation and at times obsession with the preternatural and the macabre.

In the eighteenth century, deists and their heirs sought to bring consciousness out of the sphere of myth and into the pale of science by providing a mechanical model for human psychology. In the nineteenth century with Darwin and Huxley in biology, a description of consciousness as epiphenomenon of molecular action in the brain was offered. The earlier efforts of Goethe and the poets of *Naturphilosophie*, which argued a vitalism that would have kept mind and consciousness instruments of the mythmaker, had apparently failed.

In the early years of the twentieth century, the world picture of science changed. Scientists did not give up trying to describe mind as mechanism, but the concept of mechanism itself was drastically altered. Einstein's special relativity opened the possibility that time and space are not absolute. Minkowski's subsequent application of geometric principles to Einstein's theory showed time and space as branches of one continuum. Einstein's general theory of relativity considered the matter of the universe as a curved portion of space-time.

Although Einstein himself continued to defend a deterministic universe, the quantum physicists in the 1920's offered the idea of mind as participator in any measurement in the physical universe. A basic structure could appear in two opposite and complementary forms. The work of the quantum physicists occasioned a re-examination of the phenomenon of mind which was seen to be in new ways a part of the world which had itself grown increasingly strange.

Some Western scientists and artists began to look to non-Western explications of consciousness with new concern. In the mid-twentieth century the myths of Zen Buddhism served as an acceptable mirror of the bizarre world of the new physics. The Nō dramatists viewed consciousness as a disease lost at death through the price of a sacrifice of memories in order that satori, a state of enlightenment and of emptiness, could be reached. Life for these dramatists had loveliness and great poetry. But the ultimate home of consciousness was the oblivion of the void. In the twentieth century the Japanese novelist and playwright Yukio Mishima in his modern Nō dramas and novels wrote of man's alienation from the world because of his preoccupation with beauty. Only by rejecting love of beauty and of life and by finding death could one paradoxically be liberated so that one could live.

In the later years of the twentieth century, relativistic astronomers began to speculate that the universe is even more iconoclastic than researchers had previously supposed. Astronomers spoke of black holes — apertures into nothingness — caused by the collapse of giant stars in which space-time itself would be warped, and matter might disappear forever from the visible universe.

Black holes possibly, though not probably, could open the door to intergalactic travel. Communication with other galaxies is far more probable in the future than is the possibility of travel because of the immense distances between galaxies. Hopes for a black hole "star gate" are not at this time realistic, but scientists already have the radio telescope, an instrument which makes possible the sending of intergalactic messages. Once again, scientists, at least temporarily, have found common cause with the mythmakers and have begun to explore the possibilities of intelligent life on other planets. If such life exists elsewhere in the universe, consciousness will prove to be exosomatic, not dependent on the human body.

The filmmaker Stanley Kubrick, in the script written with Arthur C. Clarke which served as a basis for Clarke's novel, has offered the possibility that human consciousness arose at the behest of extraterrestial beings possessing vastly greater development of consciousness than humans have. Kubrick and Clarke and others have also speculated on the possibility that man might some day shed the machine of his body and take consciousness to heights yet undreamed of in the myths of today or of any other day.

From the above summary, it may be seen that science and mythology may not, after all, be as diverse as they have long appeared to be. In the history of thought, the separation between these two disciplines did not at first exist. Before the Greeks, and especially in ancient Egypt and in Mesopotamia, mythology played the role not only of fiction but also of science and of philosophy.[1] In non-literate societies, mythology has the same function today. Philosophy and science are thus seen as comparatively young branches of general mythology.

The split between science and mythology which causes man to be seen both as a creature of spirit and of matter leads to far too radical a dichotomy and to a distorted picture of man. Perhaps the twentieth century will see the beginning of synthesis in the chasm which has prevented a unification of man's understanding of himself. Sir Allan Cottrell, pondering the

---

[1] For a discussion of myth as precursor to science and philosophy, see Henri Frankfort, et al., *The Intellectual Adventure of Ancient Man*, rpt. as *Before Philosophy* (1946: Harmondsworth, England: Penguin Books, 1951).

inability of physicis to acquire a vocabulary for a discussion of mind, asks:

> Is *mind* some kind of collective performance of certain very intricate atomic structures working according to the laws of physics? We know of other collective effects of atoms, not possessed by them individually, such as heat and sound, but it may be an impertinence to mention them in the same context as mind. But we have no idea at all of how matter, by physical laws, could exhibit the characteristics of mind. Certainly the laws of physics give no inkling of this. But it would be rash to suppose that we now know all or even many of the laws of nature. Like psychology and physiology today, chemistry and physics seemed separated by an unbridgeable gap a century ago: but atomic physics and the quantum theory have since brought them together as a common understanding.[2]

Perhaps scientific myths could help to bridge the gap between science and mythology and could begin to find answers to questions raised by Cottrell.

A return to the conception of consciousness along the lines of mythology is mandated by the fact that since the work of the structuralists, there has been an increasing realization that the conscious mind itself is mythical in the sense that it is not only a tentative sounding of the universe but is also a temporary ordering of the world which is practiced by humans during every waking hour of every day.

Philosophers of science since Francis Bacon have traditionally taught that science follows a rigorous method of study, hypothesis, testing, and conclusion in an attempt to keep scientific study congruent with facts. In the twentieth century Sir Karl Popper, Thomas Kuhn and others have questioned this model of scientific research. Some present-day philosophers of science hold that science is not inductive but deductive: or that science has no greater claim to validity than does fictional mythology: or that science actually allows various paradigmatic models: or that scientific theories basically are commonly held research programs which are accepted as acts of faith and are protected by various stratagems.[3]

---

[2]*Portrait of Nature* (New York: Scribner's, 1975), pp. 214-15.

[3]These problems and the philosophers who are debating these questions are the subject of Frederick Suppe, ed., *The Structure of Scientific Theories*, 2nd ed. (1973: Urbana: Univ. of Illinois Press, 1977).

In spite of the pounding which the Baconian model of scientific research has taken, most philosophers of science still consider the universe which science studies an actual entity, admittedly colored by the scientists' perceptions, but real nonetheless. Therefore the scientific hypothesis still remains for most philosophers of science the basic instrument by which scientists probe the universe, although varying conceptions of the nature, scope, and meaning of *hypothesis* continue to be under debate.

A possibility that science and myth can be reunited in a decisive step toward solving the mind/body problem can now be entertained. A new vocabulary is needed which will be able to deal with the mind and the physical world together, for while the present-day scientist continues to use hypothesis, the mythmaker when discussing consciousness produces statements of belief about the mind. The basic premise of the new critical realism is that perhaps hypotheses formed by the mind, including those dealing with self-knowledge, are structures which play a role in the mental-and-physical universe and can thus be a part of the vocabulary of the physicist as well as of the mythmaker.

A new view of nature which would combine science and myth might open the door to a better understanding of the human mind and of consciousness. There are dangers in this approach. A re-mythologized science could become stagnant. A scientific mythology could become sterile. Yet if one remembers that the human experience is not divided into tight separate compartments, a holistic approach to the study of science and of myth might dispel the anxiety of some moderns who find themselves alienated from the world. Man could reunite with his cosmos and could discover new meaning in Blake's words that nature is "one continued vision or fancy or imagination."

# BIBLIOGRAPHY

Aeschylus. *Prometheus Bound.* Trans. David Grene. 1942: rpt. in *The Complete Greek Tragedies.* Ed. David Grene and Richmond Lattimore. 4 vols. Chicago: Univ. of Chicago Press, 1959, I, 311-59.

Asimov, Isaac. *The Universe: From Flat Earth to Quasar.* New York: Walker, 1966. Paperback ed. rpt. New York: Avon Books, 1966.

Auerbach, Erich. *Mimesis: Dargestellte Wirklichkeit in Abendländischen Literatur.* Bern: Francke, 1946. Trans. Williard R. Trask as *Mimesis: The Representation of Reality in Western Literature.* Paperback ed. rpt. Princeton: Princeton Univ. Press, 1953.

Bellah, Robert. "Christianity and Symbolic Religion." *Journal for the Scientific Study of Religion,* 9(1970), 89-96.

Blake, William. *The Letters of William Blake Together With a Life by Frederick Tatham.* Ed. Archibald G.B. Russell. New York: Scribner's, 1906.

Bible. Revised Standard Version. New York: Nelson, 1952.

Bowers, Faubion. *Japanese Theatre.* New York: Hermitage House, 1952.

Bultmann, Rudolph. *The Presence of Eternity: History and Eschatology* [Published in Great Britain as *History and Eschatology*]. The Gifford Lectures. Edinburgh University, 1955. New York: Harpers, 1957.

Calder, Nigel. *The Life Game: Evolution and the New Biology.* New York: Viking, 1973. Paperback ed. rpt. New York: Dell, 1975.

Carlisle, Donald C., and Siegal, Michael I. Review of *On the Origins of Language* by Philip Lieberman. *American Journal of Physical Anthropology,* 47 (1977), 489-90.

Chaisson, Eric J. "The Scenario of Cosmic Evolution." *Harvard Magazine,* 80, No.2 (Nov.-Dec., 1977), 21-33.

Charles, R[obert] H. *A Critical History of the Doctrine of A Future Life in Israel, in Judaism, and in Christianity: Or Hebrew, Jewish and Christian Eschatology from Pre-Prophetic Times till the Close of the New Testament Canon.* 2nd ed. 1899; London: A.C. Black, 1913. Paperback ed. rpt. as *Eschatology: the Doctrine of a Future Life in Israel, Judaism, and Christianity: A Critical History.* New York: Schocken Books, 1963.

Chaucer, Geoffrey. *The Canterbury Tales*. Trans. R.M. Lumiansky. New York: Simon and Schuster, 1948.

_____. *The Canterbury Tales* [in the original Middle English]. Rpt. in Geoffrey Chaucer. *The Works of Geoffrey Chaucer*. Ed. F.N. Robinson, 1933; Boston: Houghton Mifflin, 1957.

Childs, B[revard] S. "Tree of Knowledge, Tree of Life." *The Interpreter's Dictionary of the Bible*. Ed. George Arthur Buttrick et al. 4 vols. New York: Abingdon, 1962, IV, 695-97.

Clark, [John] Grahame [D.]. *A World Prehistory: A New Outline: Being the Second Edition of "World Prehistory."* 1961; Cambridge: Cambridge University Press, 1969.

Clark, J. Desmond. "African Origins of Man the Toolmaker." *Human Origins: Louis Leakey and the East African Evidence*. Ed. Glynn Ll. Isaac and Elizabeth R. McCown. Menlo Park, Cal.: Benjamin, 1976, pp. 1-53.

Clarke, Arthur C. *The Lost Worlds of "2001."* New York: New American Library, 1972.

_____. *2001: A Space Odyssey*. New York: New American Library, 1968.

Conze, Edward. *Buddhism: Its Essence and Development*. New York: Philosophical Library. 1951. 3rd ed. New York: Harper, 1959.

Cottrell, Alan. *Portrait of Nature: The World as Seen by Modern Science*. New York: Scribner's, 1975.

Craik, K[enneth] J.W. *The Nature of Explanation*. Cambridge: Cambridge Univ. Press, 1943.

Crick, F[rancis] H.C. et al. "A Speculation on the Origin of Protein Synthesis." *Origins of Life*, 7 (1976), 389-97.

Dampier, William Cecil. *A History of Science: And Its Relations with Philosophy and Religion*. 4th ed. 1929: Cambridge: Cambridge Univ. Press, 1949.

Davies, P.C.W. *Space and Time in the Modern Universe*. Cambridge: Cambridge Univ. Press, 1977.

Desmond, Adrian J. *The Hot-Blooded Dinosaurs: A Revolution in Paleontology*. New York: Dial, 1976.

Editors of *Time*. "Why You Do What You Do: Sociobiology: A New Theory of Behavior." *Time*, 110, No. 5 (Aug. 1, 1977), 54-63.

Farb, Peter. *Humankind*. Boston: Houghton Mifflin, 1978.

Frankfort, Henri et al. *The Intellectual Adventure of Ancient Man: An Essay on Speculative Thought in the Ancient Near East*. Chicago: Univ. of Chicago Press, 1946. Rpt. as *Before Philosophy*. Harmondsworth, England: Penguin Books, 1951.

Gingrich, Owen. "Will the Universe End with a Bang or a Whimper?" *Harvard Magazine*, 79, No. 2 (July-Aug., 1977), 10-12.

Gode-von Aesch, Alexander G.F. *Natural Science in German Romanticism*. New York: Colombia Univ. Press, 1941.

Greene, William Chase. *Moira: Fate, Good and Evil in Greek Thought*. Cambridge: Harvard Univ. Press, 1944.

Hesse, Mary. *The Structure of Scientific Interference.* Berkeley: Univ. of California Press, 1974.

Homer. *The Odyssey.* Trans. Robert Fitzgerald. Garden City, New York: Doubleday, 1961.

Hoyle, Fred. "The Crisis in Astronomy." *Physics 50 Years Later: As Presented to the XIV Assembly of the International Union of Pure and Applied Physics on the Occasion of the Union's Fiftieth Anniversary, September 1972.* Ed. Sanborn C. Brown. Washington, D.C.: National Academy of Sciences, 1973, pp. 63-78.

Hughes, John P. *The Science of Language.* New York: Random House, 1962.

Hynek, J. Allen. *The UFO Experience.* Chicago: Regnery, 1972.

Isaac, Glynn Ll., and McCown, Elizabeth R., eds. *Human Origins: Louis Leakey and the East African Evidence.* Menlo Park, Cal.: Benjamin, 1976.

Jaynes, Julian. *The Origin of Consciousness in the Breakdown of the Bicameral Mind.* Boston: Houghton Mifflin, 1976.

Jerison, Harry J. *Evolution of Brain and Intelligence.* New York: Academic Press, 1973.

Kan'ami. *Sotoba Komachi.* Trans. Arthur Waley. *The Nō Plays of Japan.* New York: Knopf, 1922. Paperback ed. rpt. New York: Grove Press, 1957, pp. 148-60.

Kaufmann, William J., III. *The Cosmic Frontiers of General Relativity.* Boston: Little, Brown, 1977.

_____. *Relativity and Cosmology.* New York: Harper & Row, 1973.

Keene, Donald. *Nō: The Classical Theatre of Japan.* 1966. Paperback rev. ed. Tokyo: Kodansha International, Ltd. and New York: Harper & Row, 1973.

Keene, Donald, ed. *Twenty Plays of the Nō Theatre.* New York: Columbia Univ. Press, 1970.

Keeton, William J. *Biological Science.* 2nd ed. 1967; rpt.; New York: Norton, 1972.

Land, Edwin. "Our 'Polar Partnership' with the World Around Us." *Harvard Magazine,* 80, No. 3 (Jan.-Feb., 1978), 23-26.

Leakey, Louis S.B. *The Progress and Evolution of Man in Africa.* London: Oxford Univ. Press, 1961.

Leakey, Louis S.B., and Goodall, Vanne Morris. *Unveiling Man's Origins: Ten Decades of Thought about Human Evolution.* Boston: Schenkman, 1969.

Leakey, Richard E., and Lewin, Roger. *Origins.* New York: Dutton, 1977.

Le May, Marjorie. "The Language Capability of Neanderthal Man." *American Journal of Physical Anthropology,* 42 (1975), 9-14.

Lévi-Strauss, Claude. *Tristes Tropiques.* Paris: Plon, 1955. Trans. John Weightman and Doreen Weightman. New York: Athenium, 1974. Paperback ed. rpt. New York: Pocket Books, 1977.

Lieberman, Philip. *On the Origins of Language: An Introduction to Human Speech.* New York: Macmillan, 1975.

Lotman, Yury. (Iurii M.). *Struktura khudozhestvennogo teksta.* Moscow: "Isskustvo," 1970. Rpt. ed. Thomas G. Winner. Brown University Slavic Reprints, No. 9. Providence: Brown Univ. Press, 1971.

Lovell, Bernard. "Whence? We Are What We Know About Where We Came From." *New York Times Magazine* (Nov. 27, 1975), pp.27, 72-90, 105.

Luria, S[alvador] I. *Life: The Unfinished Experiment.* New York: Scribner's, 1973.

Mishima, Yukio. *Kinkakuji.* (1954). Trans. Ivan Morris as *The Temple of the Golden Pavilion.* New York: Knopf, 1959.

—————. *Sotoba Komachi* in *Kindai Nōgakushū* (1956). Trans. Donald Keene as *Five Modern Nō Plays.* New York: Knopf, 1957, pp. 3-34.

Monod, Jacques. *Le Hassard et la nécessité: Essai sur la philosophie naturelle de la biologie moderne.* Paris: Éditions du Seuil, 1970.

Nathan, John. *Mishima: A Biography.* Boston: Little, Brown, 1974.

Norden, Eric. "*Playboy* Interview: Stanley Kubrick." *Playboy,* 15, No. 9 (Sept., 1968), 85-96, 158, 190-95.

O'Neill, P. G. *A Guide to Nō.* Tokyo and Kyoto: Hinoki Shoten, 1953.

Oparin, Aleksandr. I. *Proizkhozhdenie zhizni [The Origin of Life].* Moscow: Izd. Moskovsky rabochy, 1924.

—————. *Vozniknovenie zhizni na zemle.* 3rd ed. 1936; Moscow: Izd. AN SSSR, 1956. Trans. Ann Synge as *The Origin of Life on Earth,* New York: Academic Press, 1957.

Pfeiffer, John E. *The Emergence of Man.* New York: Harper & Row, 1969.

Popper, Karl R. "Autobiography." in Karl R. Popper et al., *The Philosophy of Karl Popper.* Ed. Paul A. Schilpp. 2 vols. La Salle, Ill.: Open Court Publishing Co., 1974, I, 1-181.

Premack, David. *Intelligence in Ape and Man.,* Hillsdale, N.J.: Lawrence Earlbaun Associates, and New York: Halstead Press Division of Wiley, 1976.

Reps, Paul, ed. *Zen Flesh, Zen Bones: A Collection of Zen and Pre-Zen Writings.* Rutland, Vermont and Tokyo: Charles E. Tuttle Co, 1957.

Robinson, R.H. *The Buddhist Religion: A Historical Introduction.* Belmont, Cal.: Dickenson Publishing Co., 1970.

Sagan, Carl. *The Cosmic Connection: An Extraterrestial Perspective.* Garden City, New York: Doubleday, 1973. Paperback ed. rpt. New York: Dell, 1975.

Sahlins, Marshall. *The Use and Abuse of Biology.* Ann Arbor: University of Michigan Press, 1976.

Sciama, D.W. *Modern Cosmology.* Cambridge: Cambridge Univ. Press, 1971.

Shaffer, Jerome. *Philosophy of Mind.* Englewood Cliffs, N.J.: Prentice-Hall, 1968.

Shakespeare, William. *The First Part of King Henry the Fourth.* Rpt. in Shakespeare. *The Complete Works.* Ed. G.B. Harrison.

New York: Harcourt, Brace & World, 1952, pp. 617-52.

_____. *The Tragedy of Hamlet, Prince of Denmark.* Rpt. In Shakespeare. *The Complete Works.* Ed. G.B. Harrison. New York: Harcourt, Brace & World, 1952, pp. 880-932.

Shklovskii, I[osef] S. *Vselennaya, zhizn, razum.* (1962). Trans. Paula Fern and rev. Carl Sagan as *Intelligent Life in the Universe,* San Francisco: Holden-Day, 1966.

Snell, Bruno. *Die Entdeckung des Geistes.* Hamburg: Claasen und Goverts, 1946. Trans. T.G. Rosenmeyer as *The Discovery of Mind, The Greek Origins of European Thought.* Cambridge: Harvard Univ. Press, 1953.

Sophocles. *Oedipus the King.* Trans. David Grene. 1942. Rpt. in *The Complete Greek Tragedies.* Eds. David Grene and Richmond Lattimore. 4 vols.Chicago: Univ. of Chicago Press, 1959, II, 11-76.

Sturtevant, Edgar H. *An Introduction to Linguistic Science.* New Haven: Yale Univ. Press, 1947.

Suppe, Frederick, ed. *The Structure of Scientific Theories.* 2nd ed. 1973; Urbana: Univ. of Illinois Press, 1977.

Swadesh, Morris. *The Origin and Diversification of Language.* Ed. Joel Sherzer. Chicago: Aldine-Atherton, 1971.

Thorpe, W[illiam] H. *Learning and Instinct in Animals.* 2nd ed. 1956; Cambridge: Harvard Univ. Press, 1963.

Tolkien, J[ohn] R.R. "On Fairy-Stories" (1938) in Dorothy Sayers et al., *Essays Presented to Charles Williams.* London: Oxford Univ. Press, 1948. Rpt. in J.R.R. Tolkien, *Tree and Leaf.* Boston: Houghton Mifflin, 1969, pp. 1-73.

Waddington, C[onrad] H. *The Strategy of the Genes: A Discussion of Theoretical Biology.* New York: Macmillan, 1957.

_____. "The Theory of Evolution Today." in *Beyond Reductionism: New Perspectives in the Life Sciences.* Eds. Arthur Koestler and J.M. Symthes. New York: Macmillan, 1969, pp. 357-99.

Waley, Arthur, ed. *The Nō Plays of Japan.* New York: Knopf, 1922.

Wasserug, Richard. Review of *The Hot-Blooded Dinosaurs,* by Adrian S. Desmond. *Science,* 193 (1976), 44.

Weiss, Paul A. *The Science of Life: The Living System—A System for Living.* Mount Kisco, New York: Futura Publishing Co., 1973.

West, Robert H. *Shakespeare and the Outer Mystery.* Lexington: Univ. of Kentucky Press, 1968.

Wilson, Edward O. *Sociobiology.* Cambridge: Harvard Univ. Press, 1975.

Zeami. *Obasute.* Trans. Stanleigh H. Jones, Jr. as *The Deserted Crone* in *Twenty Plays of the Nō Theatre.* Ed. Donald Keene. New York: Columbia Univ. Press, 1970, pp. 115-128.

_____. *Sekidera Komachi.* Trans. Karen Brazell as *Komachi at Sekidera* in *Twenty Plays of the Nō Theatre.* Ed. Donald Keene. New York: Columbia Univ. Press, 1970, pp. 65-79.

# INDEX